Dick
Bong
America's Ace of Aces

D1567988

BOOKS BY GENERAL GEORGE C. KENNEY

General Kenney Reports

The MacArthur I Know

The Saga of Pappy Gunn

Dick Bong: Ace of Aces

Dick
Bong

America's Ace of Aces

by General George C. Kenney

With a new foreword by Marge Bong Drucker
and an introduction by Richard B. Myers,
Chairman of the Joint Chiefs of Staff

Richard I. Bong Veterans Historical Center/
Bong P-38 Fund, Inc.
Superior, Wisconsin

Dick Bong: America's Ace of Aces
Copyright © 1960 by George C. Kenney
Copyright © renewed 2003 by Richard I. Bong WWII Heritage
Center/Bong P-38 Fund, Inc.
Richard I. Bong Veterans Historical Center/Bong P-38 Fund Inc.,
305 Harbor View Parkway, Superior, WI 54880

First edition published in 1960 under the title Dick Bong: Ace of Aces
by Duell, Sloan and Pearce
Second edition published in 2003 by the Richard I. Bong WWII
Heritage Center/Bong P-38 Fund Inc.
Third edition published in 2014 by the Richard I. Bong Veterans
Historical Center/Bong P-38 Fund Inc.
Printed in the United States of America

ISBN 0-9722373-0-5

    Library of Congress Cataloging-in-Publication Data

Kenney, George C. (George Churchill), 1889-1977.
  Dick Bong : America's ace of aces / by George C. Kenney ;
with a new foreword by Marge Bong Drucker. -- 2nd ed.
    p. cm.
  ISBN 0-9722373-0-5 (pbk.)
  1. Bong, Richard I. 2. United States. Army Air Forces--Biogra-
phy. 3. Fighter pilots--United States--Biography. 4. World War,
1939-1945--Aerial operations, American. 5. World War, 1939
-1945--Pacific Area.   I. Title.
UG626.2.B66K46 2002
940.54'4973'092--dc21
[B]

2002011325

Cover painting by Herb Kawainui Kane © 2002 Richard I. Bong WWII Heritage Center
Book Design by Joy Dey

**To Major Richard Ira Bong, ace of American aces
in all of our wars, who is destined to hold that title
for all time**

WITH THE WEAPONS THAT MAN POSSESSES TODAY, no war of the future will last long enough for any pilot to run up a score of forty victories again. His country and the Air Force must never forget their number-one fighter pilot, who will inspire other fighter pilots and countless thousands of youngsters who will want to follow in his footsteps every time that any nation or coalition of nations dares to challenge our right to think, speak, and live as free people.

May this memorial building, donated by the Veterans of Foreign Wars and citizens of this community, serve as a shrine at which we may constantly resolve to see to it that we preserve our country, our ideals, and our freedom. May it also constantly remind us of our debt to our youth, which has always been willing to make any sacrifice to insure that the rest of us can keep and inherit this freedom. We owe a lot to our youth—youth typified by Dick Bong.

Today, tomorrow, and for all time, we salute you, Dick—gallant gentleman, hero, ace of aces.

—FROM THE REMARKS BY GENERAL KENNEY
AT THE DEDICATION OF THE RICHARD I. BONG MEMORIAL,
POPLAR, WISCONSIN, MAY 22, 1955

Dick Bong, Douglas MacArthur, George Kenney. PHOTO, JOHN H. STAVA COLLECTION

Foreword to the First Edition

THE AUTHOR, GENERAL GEORGE KENNEY, was my air commander during the Southwest Pacific Campaigns, which culminated in the liberation of the Philippines and the defeat of the Japanese Empire. Of all the commanders of our major Air Forces engaged in World War II, none surpassed General Kenney in those three great essentials of successful combat leadership: aggressive vision, mastery over air strategy and tactics, and the ability to exact the maximum in fighting qualities from both men and equipment. Through his capacity to improvise and improve, he took the sub-standard P-38 fighting plane and made of it a combat weapon so deadly as to take command of the air wherever it engaged the enemy against reasonable odds. It was in this type of aircraft that Major Bong achieved immortal fame as he swept the skies to victory against enemy pilots who engaged him in combat. His record has provided an imperishable inspiration to victory in all who have since or may in future rise in mortal combat to meet the challenge to American air dominance.

—DOUGLAS MACARTHUR

Dick Bong, Australia 1943. PHOTO, BONG FAMILY COLLECTION

Foreword to the Second Edition

IT IS AN HONOR AND RARE PRIVILEGE TO WRITE THE FOREWORD to this edition of the classic book *Dick Bong, Ace of Aces*, written by General George C. Kenney about my husband Major Richard Ira Bong, especially when the original foreword was written by yet another legendary figure of the World War II era, the famed General Douglas MacArthur. Bridging the time period between the first edition of March 1962 and the present gives rise again to the phrase "How fast time flies!" General Kenney gives an insightful look at the life and times of Richard and his comrades as they defended our country in the South Pacific during World War II. He writes about Richard as one who knew him well, and indeed, it has been said that Dick was one of the general's favorite "boys."

The impression that I gained about their closeness was one of almost a father-son relationship. Perhaps it was the admiration of one "hot pilot" for another. It's said that Kenney flew under the Brooklyn Bridge in World War I and was disciplined, just as Dick did under the Golden Gate Bridge in the later war. It was Kenney who persuaded MacArthur to present the Congressional Medal of Honor to Dick at Tacloban Airdrome instead of waiting to do it in Washington, D. C., where it would have been attended by more pomp and ceremony than it was on that rainy airstrip in the Pacific.

I look back on those war years with many memories—

much personal happiness and great sadness. When Richard was killed just short of six months after our wedding when he was testing one of the first fighter jets, my world turned upside down. I withdrew as much as possible from public view. I blocked out the pain of that tragedy and learned how to survive by doing so. Yet he was always a part of me . . . a first love is always special and is always held in a special place in one's heart. It took me more than forty years to return to my home state of Wisconsin. The event was the 1985 opening of The Bong Bridge spanning the twin ports of Superior and Duluth, and I was to be a part of the celebration. To my great pleasure, I received such a warm welcome that the occasion was exhilarating.

It took me another ten years to write my own book about Richard, called *Memories*. I then became totally involved with the Bong P-38 Fund, using my book and vintage pictures to raise funds all over the country for a new project: inspired by our beautifully restored P-38 Lightning we undertook to build a suitable, world-class World War II Heritage Center, sheltering our "Marge" plane and honoring Richard and all our country's World War II participants.

The present generation is only now realizing how precious are the freedoms that were handed down to them by the brave patriots of the forties who defended the United States of America without question. Newly appreciative of his lifestyle and freedoms, one youth expressed his thanks by writing, "Sorry we waited so long." Let us never take for granted the liberties we enjoy, and let us never forget the service of others that has made, and continues to make, our nation free.

—Marge Bong Drucker
September, 2002

INTRODUCTION

RICHARD I. BONG
AMERICA'S ACE OF ACES

It is a pleasure to share a few words about America's top-ranking ace and a hero among heroes, Major Richard Ira Bong. As a combat pilot who flew in Vietnam, I stand in awe of his accomplishments as well as his spirit.

While America reeled from the shock of Pearl Harbor, a pilot named Dick Bong captured the Nation's attention by flying under the Golden Gate Bridge in San Francisco. Soon, he also captured the Nation's confidence with victory after victory against the Japanese in the South Pacific. The tide began to turn for America. She was at war—and her citizens were rising to meet the challenge.

While the standard length of a tour was 25 missions, Major Bong stayed and accumulated 400 hours on 146 missions, and 40 victories over enemy pilots. He received the Congressional Medal of Honor for his heroic efforts. His record number of air combat victories will likely stand for some time.

Having also grown up as a Mid-western boy who wanted nothing more than to fly, Dick Bong's exploits inspired me. As other young Americans read this story, I hope they too are stirred to take flight.

Today, our Nation's aviators in the Air Force, Navy, Marines and Army seek to live up to the legacy of past fliers like Dick Bong. In the process, they defend our Nation and the freedoms that he and his fellow pilots defended so successfully 60 years ago.

RICHARD B. MYERS
Chairman
of the Joint Chiefs of Staff

Contents

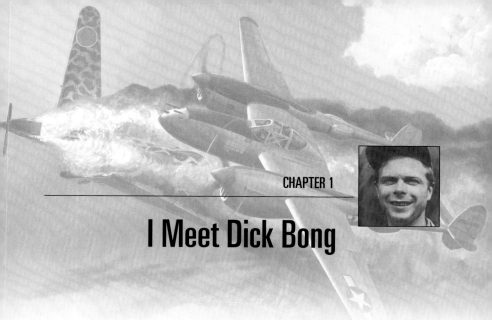

I Meet Dick Bong

MY INTRODUCTION TO DICK BONG took place in July 1942 at my headquarters in San Francisco, where I was commanding the Fourth Air Force. The circumstances were a bit unusual, to say the least. There was nothing about that meeting that even remotely indicated that two and a half years later this young man would be Major Richard Ira Bong, of the United States Army Air Force, top-scoring air ace of the war, with forty official victories to his credit and decorated with every award for valor from the Congressional Medal of Honor on down.

The Fourth Air Force was charged with the air defense of the whole Pacific coast from San Diego to Seattle, maintaining a constant offshore patrol to a distance of five hundred miles out to sea and at the same time training fighter and bomber units for service in the theaters overseas. One of my most important jobs was introducing a two-engined fighter plane called P-38 to the youngsters fresh from the individual flight-training stage. They generally came to me with no more than a hundred flying hours under their belts, all of them on single-engined aircraft. The big problem was to make combat flights, squadrons, and groups out of this material and at the same time to keep the accident rate down. The exuberance of youth in its early twenties must not be stifled, but there had to be enough discipline to keep the "wild blue yonder" fliers from killing themselves as well as to prevent them from annoying the local inhabitants and giving the Air Force a black eye.

I had just finished reading a long report concerning the exploits of one of my young pilots who had been looping the loop around the center span of the Golden Gate Bridge in a P-38 fighter plane and waving to the stenographic help in the office buildings as he flew along Market Street. The report noted that, while it had been extremely difficult to get information from the somewhat sympathetic and probably conniving witnesses, there was plenty of evidence indicating that a large part of that waving had been to people on some of the lower floors of the buildings. Streetcars had stopped, taxis had run up on the sidewalks, and pedestrians had fled to the nearest doorways to get indoors and under cover. There was even a rumor that the insurance companies were contemplating raising the rates. The fire and police departments both seemed quite concerned.

A woman on the outskirts of Oakland was quoted as saying that she didn't need any help from fighter pilots in removing her washing from the clotheslines unless they would like to do it on the ground. I told my secretary to get her address and telephone number and tell her that I would see to it that she wouldn't be bothered any more.

Considering the mass of evidence, it was surprising that more complaints had not been registered, but in any event I would have to do something about the matter. Washington was determined to stop low-altitude stunting and had put out some stringent instructions about how to handle the budding young aviators who broke the rules. The investigation officer had recommended a general court-martial. If found guilty, the culprit would be dismissed from the Air Force but could still be drafted into the infantry. He could even be sentenced to a term in a federal penitentiary.

I had sent word to the pilot's commanding officer that I wanted to see the lad in my office, and I was expecting him at any minute. I had just decided to be really tough with him and had pretty well worked myself up to that frame of mind, when my secretary opened the door and said, "Your bad boy is outside. You remember—the one you wanted to see about flying around bridges and down Market Street."

As rough and gruff as I could make it, and loud enough so that I was sure he could hear me, I said, "Send him in." I heard her say, "The General will see you now, Lieutenant," and in walked one of the nicest-looking cherubs you ever saw in your life. I suspected that he was not over twenty and maybe even younger. I doubted if he was old enough to shave. He was just a little blond-haired Swedish boy about five feet six, with a round, pink baby face and the bluest, most innocent eyes—now opened wide and a bit scared. Someone must have told him how serious this court-martial thing might be. He wanted to fly and he wanted to get into the war and do his stuff, but now he was finding out that they were really tough about this low-altitude "buzzing" business, and it was dawning on him that the commanders all had orders really to bear down on young aviators who looped around bridges, flew down city streets, and rattled dishes in people's houses. Why, he might be taken off flying status or even thrown out of the Air Force! He wasn't going to alibi out of it, but he sure hoped this General Kenney wasn't going to be too tough. You could actually see all the stuff going on in his head just behind those baby-blue eyes. He didn't know it, but he had already won.

I let him stand at attention while I bawled him out for getting himself in trouble and getting me in trouble, too, besides giving people the impression that the Air Force was just a bunch of irresponsible airplane jockeys. He could see that he was in trouble just by looking at the size and thickness of the pile of papers on my desk that referred to his case. But think of all the trouble he had made for me. Now, in order to quiet down the people who didn't approve of his exuberance, I would have to talk to the governor, the mayor, the chief of police. Luckily, I knew a lot of people in San Francisco who could be talked into a state of forgiveness, but I had the job of looking after the Fourth Air Force, and I should spend my time doing that instead of running around explaining away the indiscretion of my wild-eyed pilots.

"By the way, wasn't the air pretty rough down in that street around the second-story level?" I was really a bit curious. As I remembered, it used to be when I was first learning to fly.

"Yes, sir, it was kind of rough," replied the cherub, "but it was easy to control the plane. The aileron control is good in the P-38 and . . ." He paused. Probably figured he had said enough. For a second the blue eyes had been interested more than scared. He was talking about his profession, and it was more than interest. It was his life, his ambition. I would bet anything that he was an expert in a P-38 and that he wanted to be still better. We needed kids like this lad.

"Lieutenant," I said, "there is no need for me to tell you again that this is a serious matter. If you didn't want to loop around that bridge or fly down Market Street, I wouldn't have you in my Air Force, but you are not going to do it any more, and I mean what I say. From now on, if I hear any more reports of this kind about you, I'll put you before a general court, and if they should recommend dismissal from the service, which they probably would, I'll approve it."

I began slowly to tear up the report and drop the pieces

of paper in the wastebasket. The blue eyes watched, a little puzzled at first, and then the scared look began to die out. I growled at him again. It wouldn't do to let him get unscared too soon.

"Monday morning you check in at this address out in Oakland, and if that woman has any washing to be hung out on the line, you do it for her. Then you hang around being useful—mowing a lawn or something—and when the clothes are dry, take them into the house. And don't drop any of them on the ground or you will have to wash them over again. I want that woman to think we are good for something besides annoying people. I am going to tell her that you will be there at seven thirty, so you'd better show. Now get out of here quick before I get mad and change my mind. That's all."

"Yes, sir." He didn't dare to change his expression, but the blue eyes had gone all soft and relieved. He saluted and backed out of the office.

The door closed and I settled back in my chair thinking how wonderful it would be to be a kid in my twenties again, flying a "hot" airplane like the P-38, instead of being fifty-two and a general commanding a whole Air Force and riding herd on a lot of wonderful, enthusiastic, sparkling young pilots who had caught the same fever that I had twenty-five years before. I could still see those bridges over New York's East River, flashing by overhead on my first solo flight, back in the summer of 1917, and I could almost hear again the bawling out that I got from the colonel commanding the field a couple of hours after I landed. For a while it had looked as though I was going to be fired out of aviation and sent back to be drafted into the infantry, but the intervention of my civilian instructor, and the already famous Bert Acosta, and the tolerance of Colonel "Mike" Kilner, my commanding officer, had allowed me to stay in the flying game and grow up to be a general. Mike had been a nice guy to me, and I had always appreciated it. I hoped that in following his example I was also being a nice guy and that this towheaded youngster would also grow up to be a general someday.

My reveries were interrupted by the light flashing on the direct telephone line from my desk to General Henry H. "Hap" Arnold, the head of the Army Air Forces in Washington. We were close personal friends of more than twenty years' standing and had worked together through all the growing pains that aviation had gone through before being recognized as a legitimate part of the military organization by the big brass of the Army and the Navy. We used to have lots of arguments, but we understood each other. Hap used to call me his "trouble shooter," and the jobs that I had done for him for years had been of that variety. I wondered what was on his mind now.

"George, pack up and come to Washington. Be in my

office at eight o'clock Monday morning. I'll give you all the dope then. I can't tell you any more on the telephone. Oh, yes, and let me know who you want to recommend to take over your job."

I took off for Washington that afternoon, wondering what my new assignment was to be and where I was going. The only things I could be sure of were that Hap was in a hurry about something and that it undoubtedly was another trouble-shooting job.

My estimate of the situation turned out to be right. General Douglas MacArthur, commanding the Allied Forces in the Southwest Pacific Theater, had asked for me to come out there right away and take over command of the Allied Air Force in the theater, and it was a real number-one trouble-shooting job.

Japanese aviation not only outnumbered the combined American and Australian Air Forces, but the Jap pilots, who averaged around six or seven hundred flying hours of experience apiece, were equipped with excellent aircraft of all types. As a result, they dominated the air over the main combat area of New Guinea, and their bombers and fighters raided Darwin and other ports in northern Australia almost at will. Our Air Force units were far below strength and were flying airplanes that were worn out from combat use and lack of spare parts and replacements. The morale of both flying and ground crews was at a low ebb.

I spent a few days in Washington studying the situation and getting instructions from General George Marshall, the Army Chief of Staff, and General Arnold. Everyone in Washington seemed to think that the Japs were about to run the Allies out of New Guinea and that we would soon be fighting in Australia. When I mentioned a little higher priority than last place for some more airplanes and crews, I was reminded that the Southwest Pacific Theater was to be a defensive theater until the European situation was straightened out and that the answer to my request was "No." However, I did finally argue Hap into one concession. He had never been too keen about the P-38 as a fighter plane. He and most of the fighter people in his headquarters were prejudiced against a two-engined fighter plane as it would not have quite the maneuverability of a single-engined job. On the other hand, the P-38 had twice the range of any other fighter in the Air Force; it would out-climb and out-speed them; and furthermore, it would fly on one engine. That feature looked good to me for work in the Pacific where the distances were great and most of the flying would be over water or jungle country.

I really think he was glad to get rid of them or maybe it was just to get rid of me, but whatever the reason, Hap finally said he would let me have fifty P-38s and my pick of fifty of the pilots I had trained out on the West Coast. The list of names I submitted to him before I left Washington on my way to Australia was headed by my stunt-flying bad boy, Second Lieutenant Richard I. Bong.

P-38s in formation. PHOTO, U.S. AIR FORCE

CHAPTER 2

From Farm Boy to Fighter Pilot

RICHARD IRA BONG WAS BORN IN SUPERIOR, WISCONSIN, on September 24, 1920.

His father, Carl T. Bong, came to America in 1898 at the age of seven with his mother, a brother, and two sisters, from Islingby, Domnarvet, Dalarna, Sweden. His grandfather, Gust Bong, had preceded them by a couple of years and had settled on a small farm in Poplar, a little town of around four hundred people, twenty miles southeast of Superior.

Carl grew up like the average farm boy of those days. School, working on the farm for his father, hunting, and fishing took care of his schedule during the spring, summer, and fall. In the winter, there was logging to be done as soon as there was enough snow to use the sleds to bring out timber for construction and firewood to feed the stoves that did the double duty of cooking and heating. As he got older, there was another job for him. Every family had to do its share of putting the roads in shape after the spring thaws were over. It was while he was working along Highway 2 just outside of Poplar that one afternoon he noticed an attractive little brunette walking home from school. Judicious inquiries established that her name was Dora Bryce, the daughter of a farmer on the other side of town. In a community predominantly Scandinavian, she was of Scotch-English descent with a touch of Irish on her grandmother's side. It didn't take too long to arrange that her arrival coincided with the time that he was through work for the day and available to escort her home and soon to have a steady evening date as well.

The wedding took place in Duluth, Minnesota, July 29, 1919. It would have been a couple of years earlier, but when World War I broke out in April 1917, Carl went into the Army. They both agreed the marriage should wait until the war was over. Besides, Dora was not quite seventeen. After a tour in France, Carl came home in July 1919 to be demobilized in Duluth. He was now twenty-eight. They settled in Poplar, which is still the family home.

Richard, the first of nine children, was born the following year. He was named after two uncles: Richard, after his father's baby brother, who had died at the age of two, and Ira, for Ira Wiley, an uncle by marriage who was married to his grandmother Bryce's sister.

In 1928 President Calvin Coolidge was vacationing and fishing at the Cedar Island estate on the Brule River not far from Superior, where he had established the summer White

House office at the Superior Central High School. His mail came in daily by Army airplane, which flew directly over the Bong farm. As he watched them, Dick, then eight years old, began dreaming of the day when he would be a flier. From the very first, he wanted to pilot a fast single-seater. He was going to be a fighter pilot.

It wasn't long before he and a school chum, Roger Robinson, began making model planes, and from then on there were always two or three hanging from the ceiling of Dick's bedroom, which he shared with his younger brother Carl. Dick's models were almost always fighter planes. Roger liked the bomber types. When there was a birthday or some such party at the Bong home, in a few minutes Dick and Roger would be missing. If anyone was interested in looking for them, they would be found upstairs working on their airplanes or talking about flying.

Dick got his first gun, a .22 rifle, when he was twelve. It was meant to be a surprise birthday present. Dora and Carl were both looking forward to the event and anticipating the lad's reaction when they gave him the one thing that he wanted more than anything else. His father, who had been teaching him how to shoot for several years, handed it to his son and proudly watched as the boy threw the rifle up to his shoulder and squinted along the barrel like a veteran. Now he had his own gun and could join the fall deer hunts then so popular in northern Wisconsin. Besides his father, there were his uncles, Henning, Roy, Hank, and Arvid, all Bongs and his cousins Alec and Bill Bong. In his own age group, there were the three Erickson boys, the Edquist twins, Albert and Melvin, and Erland Bjork, all neighbors in Poplar.

During the hunting season, this mob congregated at the Bong household every morning, long before dawn, and noisily talked over the hits and misses of the previous day and where they were going to hunt on that particular day. Although the Bongs were all good shots and kept the house well supplied with venison, Dora and the rest of the family heaved sighs of relief when the season was over and they could at least sleep until sunup.

Dick attended grade school and high school at Poplar. As Poplar High School only taught three grades, he completed his senior year at the Superior Central High School in the summer of 1938, finishing fourteenth in the graduating class of four hundred.

Besides being a model student, Dick played on the school baseball, basketball, and hockey teams, was an excellent bowler, played a clarinet in both high-school bands, sang in the Lutheran Church choir, was active in the 4-H club, and did his share of hunting and fishing. One of his 4-H projects was planting a row of evergreen trees along the west boundary of the farm. They are now beautiful tall trees that form a fine wind and snow barrier near the Bong home.

Everyone who knew him in those days agrees that Dick

was a fine, likable youngster belonging to a nice, well-brought-up, close-knit family. Between school terms, he worked on his father's farm. If it hadn't been for the combination of airplanes and a war, he probably would have been a farmer, and a good one. He didn't smoke or drink. He didn't avoid girls, but making model airplanes occupied many more of his evenings than his occasional dates. The only times he ever seems to have worried his family was when he got his hands on the steering wheel of a car or a truck. He kept both in excellent shape, but when he drove either of them, he liked to push the foot throttle all the way to the floor.

After graduating from the Superior Central High School in 1938, Dick entered State Teachers College in Superior, but aviation kept calling him, and on May 29, 1941, he enlisted in the Army Air Force as a flying cadet and was ordered to Tulare, California, for the primary flight training course, which he completed on August 16, 1941. His next station was Gardner Field near Taft, California, for the basic-training phase, which he finished on November 4, 1941. Luke Field, near Phoenix, Arizona, then provided him with the final advanced, single-engine, pilot-training course. He graduated on January 9, 1942, got his pilot's wings, and was commissioned on that date as a second lieutenant in the Army Air Force Reserve. He had realized his ambition. He was now a fighter pilot.

His commanding officer at Luke Field was Brigadier

General Ennis C. Whitehead, under whom he was to serve in the Pacific later on. Whitehead says of Dick's ability:

"Dick Bong was in one of the early classes at Luke Field. He made the best score in the rather limited gunnery training, which we conducted on ground targets and on towed targets with AT-6 advanced trainers carrying one caliber-30 machine gun mounted in each wing.

Dick Bong, second row far left, poses with 49th Fighter Squadron in early 1942. PHOTO, MRS. CHARLES EARNHART

"Bong could simply fly an AT-6 better than his contemporaries and for that reason made a much better score on tow targets. He was good enough so that we kept him as an instructor for several months. He was a good one."

By this time, we were in the war against Germany and Japan and every one of the youngsters hoped for a combat assignment as soon as they finished training. Much to his disgust at the time, Dick now found himself assigned as an instructor at Luke Field. However, he philosophically accepted his new role. At least he could get in lots of flying and improve his aerial gunnery so that if he did get into combat, he would be better equipped for the job. Actually, the three and a half months he spent at Luke Field were to prove invaluable to him later on. When he was assigned to me at Hamilton Field, California, on May 1, 1942, Whitehead wrote me that I was getting one of the hottest pilots he had seen in years. He also mentioned another young pilot whom he had kept as an instructor, named Gerald Johnson. We were destined to hear from him, too. So were the Japs.

PILOTS of
?th Fighter Squadron of

After four months at Hamilton Field flying P-38s, and behaving as a first-class fighter pilot should, except for a little unauthorized flying around bridges and down San Francisco streets, Dick was shipped to Australia by Hap Arnold, who kept his promise to me. He reported to me in Brisbane on September 10, 1942. I assigned him to a P-38 squadron that was just beginning to assemble its newly arrived airplanes. It was the Ninth Squadron of the Forty-ninth Fighter Group of the Fifth Air Force.

CHAPTER 3

First Victory

JUST BEFORE THANKSGIVING, Eddie Rickenbacker arrived in Australia. He still looked thin and worn from spending three weeks floating around in a rubber boat, after the B-17 in which he was flying got lost, ran out of fuel, and had to ditch somewhere in the Pacific southwest of Canton Island. The Navy rescued him and had done their best to fatten him up for a couple of weeks but "Rick" was too restless by nature to sit still. He was on an inspection mission for the Secretary of War, and he wanted to get on with it. As soon as he found that the war was in New Guinea, not in Australia, New Guinea was where he wanted to go. The next morning we flew him up to Port Moresby.

We spent the afternoon at Fifth Air Force Headquarters with General Whitehead, who commanded my forward echelon in New Guinea, General Walker, who headed the Fifth Bomber Command, and some of the staff, talking about the war. Eddie was dumbfounded to learn that we were operating on the thinnest of shoestrings. None of our squadrons were at more than half strength; we were short of spare parts, engines, and supplies of all kinds.

19

We never seemed to have any more than two or three days' supply of gasoline, bombs, and ammunition on hand. The climate was hot and steaming. It was jungle country with all its bugs and tropical disease, and worst of all, there was almost a complete lack of such things as fresh meat and vegetables. Everything came out of a can, and sometimes the cannery had done a bad job.

We discussed our tactics as well as those of the Japs and the new methods that we had to invent to cope with an enemy who outnumbered us in aircraft by at least two to one. It reminded us of the early days back in World War I when we first met superior numbers of German aviators in France.

I then drove Eddie over to Government House, General MacArthur's forward headquarters, where he was to stay as a guest while in New Guinea. We had our Thanksgiving dinner that evening. Following the meal, MacArthur gave him the story of the local army situation and the general picture of what was going on in the Southwest Pacific Area.

The next day, Eddie and I toured airdromes all day and talked with the kids. Rick was still the number-one American ace and World War I hero to the fighter pilots. After a lot of discussion about air-combat tactics, one of the youngsters said, "Captain Rickenbacker, how many victories did you have in the last war?"

Rick told him the number was twenty-six. Quite a few of the kids said something about having only two or three or maybe only one, and they guessed that the number twenty-six would stand for a long while to come.

"There is something else about that score that is worth remembering," I said. "Captain Rickenbacker shot down those twenty-six German planes between June 1 and November 11 the same year of 1918."

Almost apologetically, Eddie remarked, "Well, of course you have to remember that the Germans were pretty thick on the front in those days. There were always plenty of targets to shoot at."

No one said anything for a few seconds, and then Dick Bong, who hadn't opened his mouth up to this time, drawled, "Captain Rickenbacker, the Japs are pretty thick over here, too."

We all laughed, and then I got what I thought at the time was a bright idea.

"Eddie," I said, "I'm going to give a case of scotch to the first one to beat your old record."

Eddie immediately chimed in, "Put me down for another case."

We left amid a lot of grins, but twenty-six was still a long way off. Captain "Buzz" Wagner's eight, which he had when he left to go back home a couple of months before, still headed the list.

That night at dinner with General MacArthur, we told him of the offers we had made. The general smiled and remarked that after drinking all that whisky a man ought to have something to taper off on and that maybe we should add a case of champagne for the purpose.

The next day the story was all over New Guinea.

I don't think any of us realized at the time what our scheme was destined to lead to and the adverse comments we were to get from home. The kids all thought it was a wonderful idea. It wasn't going to make them try any harder, but it added a bit of levity to the conversation and helped take some of the grim seriousness out of the business of fighting a tough war under primitive conditions in a miserable climate against a skilled and ruthless opponent. Later on, however, we were to find that some people back home didn't look upon our efforts to keep up the morale of our fighting men with the same viewpoint that we had.

A couple of days later I flew Eddie back to Brisbane where he was to stay for about a week before going home.

The P-38s had been in New Guinea since the middle of September, but we had been having constant trouble with leaking cooling systems and had been forced practically to rebuild the wings. Then the bulletproof fuel tanks had come apart at the seams and we had to wait for an emergency shipment from the United States. A few limited patrols were all that we could manage until the last week in December, when the P-38s got what they had been looking for—a good fight. Twelve of them were on alert at Laloki strip, one of our fighter fields just outside of Port Moresby, when we got the radar warning of an approaching Jap formation.

Captain Tommy Lynch led the show off the ground, and twenty minutes from take-off the twelve P-38s were at 18,000 feet, one hundred and twenty-five miles away, over Dobodura on the north coast of Papua, where they made their interception with twenty-five Jap fighters and bombers. Just as they crossed the Owen Stanley Mountains, some P-40 fighters returning to Port Moresby, at about 7,000 feet, escorting some cargo planes, called over the radio, "Hey, P-38s, bandits coming in to Dobo 18,000 feet up." Lynch called back, "O.K., P-40s thanks. We'll drive a few down to your level."

They got fifteen out of the twenty-five Jap planes. Lynch shot down two; a little towheaded, pink-cheeked kid named Second Lieutenant Richard I. Bong, my former bad boy from San Francisco, got two; and a Lieutenant Ken Sparks got a couple. We had no losses.

I went over to the squadron headquarters when they returned to congratulate the gang, hear the stories, and read their reports. They were priceless. Most of them were long and detailed, describing every maneuver and shot fired. In some of them, you could almost see the writer strut. Dick Bong's report, however, simply gave his time of take-off, the time of arrival over Dobodura, his altitude, the fact that he had shot down two Japanese airplanes, the first one a fighter and the second a bomber, and the time of arrival back at Laloki strip.

From their descriptions of the fight, most of them did everything wrong. They opened fire too far away, they tried maneuver combat with the Jap fighter that we called the Zero, which could outmaneuver them, and just got excited in their

Dick Bong in March 1943. PHOTO, U.S. AIR FORCE

first encounter. Luckily the Japs were evidently surprised in this, their first meeting with the P-38s, which were faster and could out-climb anything they had. I pretended to get mad and gave them the devil. Then I turned to George Prentice, the squadron commander, and said, "Huh, I'll bet you haven't even got any liquor to celebrate your first combat." Prentice said he hadn't, so I said, "There you are, robbing me of my

only three bottles of scotch." I turned over to them three bottles that "Mac" Laddon of Consolidated Aircraft had sent me as a Christmas present and that had just arrived that morning. I sent word to Bob Gross of the Lockheed Company, which made the P-38, that he owed Laddon three bottles and me three bottles for turning mine in to celebrate a Lockheed victory.

That evening, Whitehead and I were discussing the fight. I said, "Watch that boy Bong. There is the top American ace of aces of this war. He just started to work today."

Whitehead liked Tommy Lynch. Lynch was a wonderful youngster and a sweet combat leader, but I guessed that he would tire long before that cool little Scandinavian boy, Bong. I had only one reservation. If Dick ever realized that he was shooting people instead of clay pigeons, I believed that I would pull him out of combat. This was a nice kid, and I hated to think that someday he might hurt an awful lot when he found out that war was a dirty business.

Eddie Rickenbacker sent me a message the next day: "Hearty congratulations on your swell day, but why in hell did you wait until I left."

I think General MacArthur got as much kick out of the fight as anyone on New Guinea. He had met all the pilots in the squadron and he strongly hinted that I should be putting out some decorations unless I wanted him to do the job for me.

CHAPTER 4

The Score Mounts

ON JANUARY 7, 1943, while Bong's squadron was escorting our bombers, attacking an enemy convoy of ships in Huon Gulf, which were headed for Lae—the Japanese-held port on the north coast of New Guinea—Bong added two Nip Zero fighters to his score, and the following day, over Lae, shot down another fighter to become a full-fledged ace. I gave him and Captain Tommy Lynch, who had boosted his score to six during those two days, a couple of weeks' leave in Australia, where they could rest, get some decent food, and forget about the war for a while.

Except for one big day on February 6, when during an attempted enemy air raid on our airdromes around Dobodura, we got twenty-five out of forty Nip fighters and bombers with no losses to ourselves, the Japs kept pretty well out of the air over New Guinea for the next few weeks, which was lucky for us, as our P-38s were still giving us trouble, as we tried to keep them in flying condition.

On March 3, the opening day of the Battle of the Bismarck Sea, while covering our bombers attacking the Jap convoy off Finschhafen, Dick got his sixth official victory, his first with the Ninth fighter Squadron. The first five came while he was temporarily assigned to the 39th Fighter Squadron for additional training. I took off for Washington the next day and did not return until April 6. During my absence, I found that Bong had added two more Jap fighter planes to his score on March 11 and a bomber, his ninth, on March 29. I ordered him promoted to the rank of first lieutenant as of the day I got back. On April 14, the Japs came down from their base at Rabaul, on the island of New Britain, with a formation of thirty-seven bombers, twenty-five dive bombers, and thirty fighters, to work on our shipping in Milne Bay on the eastern end of New Guinea.

We intercepted with forty-two fighters, eight of which were P-38s. One of these was flown by Dick Bong , who got one of the Jap bombers, making him a double ace with ten confirmed victories.

The raid was the third in three days made by enemy formations of around seventy to one hundred planes each. The three raids had cost the Japs at least sixty planes. Photographs of the airdromes around Rabaul on the fifteenth showed that the remainder of what had been a special task force had flown back to its home airdromes at Truk in the Carolines.

I was glad that they had gone. Our fighters' strength was getting lower and lower. We didn't have the spare parts to repair airplanes or spare engines to replace those worn out in combat. We really were lucky that the Japs didn't know enough to take advantage of the fix we were in. It wasn't until the twelfth of June that the Nips came close enough for a fight. Then it was only a reconnaissance plane escorted by a couple of fighters. A flight of four P-38s picked them up about fifty miles northwest of Lae and got all three of them. Bong shot down one of the fighters. Score—eleven.

On June 20, at my headquarters in Brisbane, Lieutenant Colonel Neel Kearby, a short, slight, good-looking, black-haired Texan, about thirty-two, reported to me for duty. He had just arrived in command of a new group of P-47s that Arnold had promised me when I was back in Washington three months before. This keen-eyed lad looked and sounded like money in the bank to me. About two minutes after he had introduced himself he wanted to know who had the highest scores for shooting down Jap aircraft. You could sense that he just wanted to know who he had to beat and that there was no doubt in his mind who was going to be top man if we would just show him where the Japs were and let him at them. I told him that he would have plenty of opportunities as soon as we could get his P-47s off the boat and erect them.

It was more than a month before Bong got a chance to boost his score again. This time, on July 26, he really did a job. One flight of eight P-38s shot down eleven Jap fighters out of sixteen trying to interfere with our bombing raid on Lae. Four Jap fighters fell to Dick's guns in that argument.

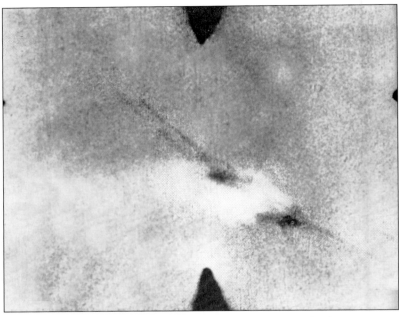

Bong's gun camera shows a Jap plane being destroyed. This picture was taken on March 15, 1943, when Dick Bong was flying a P-38 of the 9th Fighter Squadron. It shows a Jap twin-engine reconnaissance bomber, known as a Dinah, being shot down.
PHOTO, U.S. AIR FORCE

The score had now jumped to fifteen, one behind the top score held by Tommy Lynch, whom I had promoted to major and sent home for a much-needed rest the week before. When I got the news about Bong's quartet of victories in a single fight, I awarded him a Distinguished Service Cross and promoted him to captain.

Two days later a flight of nine P-38s shot down eight

more fighters. One was credited to Dick Bong. He was now tied with Lynch at sixteen.

During the melee, Bong noticed a Jap fighter diving after a P-38 that had lost one of its engines. The P-38 pilot was headed for some clouds a few hundred yards away, attempting to get under cover and try to work his way home on the remaining engine. Dick quickly estimated the situation. It looked to him as thought the Jap would catch up with the crippled P-38 before it could reach the cloud cover. Dick turned and cut in back of the cripple, which made him a closer target for the Jap than the cripple. Further to entice the Nip, he calmly feathered one of his engines so it looked as though he, too, were flying on only one engine. He then put on an exhibition of single-engined performance that must have been something for the record book. In a few minutes, he saw his pal had reached the cloud cover, so he started up his dead engine, thumbed his nose at the Jap, and left him behind. With both engines operating, our P-38 was faster than any Jap fighter plane.

Pretty soon, Dick's airplane began to vibrate badly. Looking back, Bong saw that about half his tail surface was gone. The Jap was nowhere in sight, so Dick throttled down and headed for our nearest field, just opened at Marilinan, fifty miles west of Lae. The vibration quieted, and arriving over the field, Bong shot for a landing.

Now he found that not only half his tail was gone but

his ailerons were badly damaged. He still managed to keep the P-38 on even keel, but when his wheels touched, he realized that he had no brakes and one tire had been punctured. He finally wound up in a ditch beyond the end of the runway, and his P-38 was a total loss. The worst of it was that I had no replacement and wouldn't get another plane for him for another couple of months. When we dragged the wreck in to salvage it for spare parts, we decided that only a miracle had allowed Bong to bring it back. The armor-plate shield that protected his back and head was pitted with a score of dents that looked as though someone had been hammering on a soft steel plate with a ball-pointed hammer. There were at least fifty bullet holes in the fuselage and wings. Some of the shots had barely missed the control cables. Both main fuel tanks were punctured, but the self-sealing rubber covering had prevented leakage and saved him from burning up.

Bong hated to lost his airplane, but he treated the whole affair as a huge joke on the Jap. He said, "Boy, I'll bet that guy wondered what kept that P-38 flying, and he sure must have been mad when he saw that I had foxed him into thinking I had only one engine."

That afternoon, one of Bong's wingmen came to me with a complaint. He said, "General, you've got to do something about Bong. He's giving away Nips." I asked him what he meant.

"Well, sir" replied the lad, "it's this way. Today in that fight over Cape Gloucester, I followed Bong down on a bunch of Zeros. He fired a burst into one of them, and as he jumped for another, he called to me to finish off that first Nip. Without thinking, I fired, but as I did, I saw that the Jap's wing was coming off, and the whole plane was on fire. When we got back and were starting to write up our reports, he said, 'I saw your Nip crash on that coral reef just to the north of the Cape. I'll certify to it for you.' 'Listen, Dick,' I said, 'that's your Nip. He was already gone, with a wing falling off and on fire when I hit him.' 'Oh, no,' says Bong, 'he's yours. I just grazed him. He probably would have gotten away if you hadn't finished him off. You have to make sure, because a lot of times they'll get away if you don't.' General, please tell me what I ought to do. He says if I don't take that Nip, nobody will. He wrote in his report that I got it, and he's really stubborn about the whole thing. This business today is not the only time he's given away Nips either. Every wingman he's ever had will tell you the same thing."

I told him not to come to me with his troubles and to pass the word to the others that such matters were between them and Bong. The job of being a wingman for an aggressive, hot pilot, like Dick, was not an easy one, and the casualty rate was high. If Bong believed that his wingman was partly responsible for his victories, there was nothing wrong with sharing them with the man who protected his tail and helped him shoot down Japs. The youngster left, not wholly convinced, but at least knowing that while I wouldn't get into the argument, it was quite evident that I approved of Bong's action.

I had heard such stories before. In fact, I still am certain that Dick certified at least one victory to his wingmen for every two that he reported for himself.

On that same day, Neel Kearby moved his P-47 group up to Port Moresby, but as the airplanes had arrived from the United States without any auxiliary fuel tanks, Neel and his gang were restricted to local defense missions until they could carry enough fuel to go where the Japs were. By this time, except for the occasional night bomber, it was a rare thing for a Japanese airplane to fly anywhere near Port Moresby. Ford of Australia had promised delivery of two hundred auxilary tanks by August 15. Until then, Kearby would have to forget about running up a score.

On the afternoon of September 4, Kearby's group and a flight of P-38s were flying cover for our landing craft returning from depositing the Ninth Australian Division on Hopoi Beach for an assault on the port of Lae about ten miles to the west. A Jap formation of around a hundred fighters and bombers attempted to attack our shipping. It cost them twenty-three aircraft. We lost two P-38s and two of the landing craft were damaged. Kearby and his wingman spotted a Jap bomber and a fighter flying close together about four thousand feet below them. The two P-47s, with Neel leading, dived to the attack. Kearby lined up the two Nip airplanes in his sights, fired one long burst, and got them both. A wing tore off the fighter, and the bomber exploded before the astonished wingman could get in a shot. The race was on. By the end of the month Neel had eight Jap planes to his credit. Bong with his score of sixteen was out in front, but he still didn't have an airplane. He was down at Brisbane waiting for one to be assembled from a shipment that had just come in. I had promised him the first one to be erected. He didn't seem to worry about anyone else's score. He just was not in a race. I told him that when he got his score up to twenty, I would give him a couple of months' leave to go home to Wisconsin and shoot at some deer instead of Japs. Dick grinned, and said, "If I can get me a plane, I ought to make it by the middle of November when the season opens."

He got his plane the next morning and took off for New Guinea, arriving just in time to join his squadron, which was escorting a bombing raid on the Jap airdrome at Gasmata, on the south coast of the island of New Britain. No opposition was encountered, but Bong spotted a Japanese reconnaissance plane just as the bombing formation had completed its mission and was turning around to go home. He dived to the attack, fired a long burst, and the score became seventeen.

Kearby made a herculean effort to close the gap nine days later. During the attacks on the four Jap airdromes in the Wewak area during late August and early September, we had reduced the Jap air strength there to practically zero.

The runways were badly pitted and our reconnaissance showed activity to be at a standstill. To make doubly sure, however, we ran a patrol of a flight of fighters up there every day to see if the Japs intended to become active again.

Neel decided that this was a good way for him and members of his group staff to keep their hands in. Kearby had already established himself as a superb shot and combat leader, even in the short time he had been in the theater, but on October 11 he set a real mark for the boys to shoot at. With three other pilots from his own headquarters staff, he was making a sweep over Wewak when he sighted a single Jap plane below him. Kearby, followed by his "Three Musketeers," promptly dived on the Nip and shot him down in flames. As the quartet pulled up, they sighted a Jap formation of thirty-three bombers and twelve fighters dead ahead. Without hesitating, Kearby gave the signal for an attack. Plunging into the midst of the enemy, he quickly shot down three planes, then reversed his course and knocked down two more that were on the tail of one of his wingmen. Neel then pulled off to one side and, seeing one of his formation threatened by a Jap fighter diving from above, made a final pass, practically cutting the enemy airplane in two with one burst from his eight .50-caliber guns. With his plane getting low on fuel, he then reformed his flight and led it safely home. The other three had each gotten a victory apiece and the remainder of the Jap formation had turned and was headed back west as our fighter patrol left the area.

Kearby came to my headquarters soon after he landed and told the story of the fight. General MacArthur had come over to talk with me about a big strike I was planning against Rabaul in a few weeks. I remarked to him that the record number of official victories in a single fight so far was five, credited to one of the Navy pilots over the Solomons, and that he had been awarded a Medal of Honor for the action. I added that as soon as I could get witnesses' statements from the other three pilots and see the combat camera-gun pictures, if the evidence proved that Kearby had gotten five or more Nips I wanted to recommend him for the same decoration. The general said he would approve it and send it to Washington, recommending the award. We both congratulated Kearby, and I left for Fighter Command Headquarters to get the evidence.

The testimony of the other three members of this flight and the camera-gun pictures confirmed the first six victories beyond a doubt. At the time Kearby got the seventh, however, the other three pilots had been so absorbed in extricating themselves from combat that they had not watched his last fight, and much to my disgust, the camera gun had run out of film just as it showed Kearby's tracer bullets begin to hit the nose of the Jap plane. I wrathfully wanted to know why the photographic people hadn't loaded enough film, but they apologetically explained that this was the first time anyone had ever used that much. They hadn't realized that enough film to record seven separate victories was necessary, but from now on they would see that Colonel Kearby had enough for ten Japs.

I put in the recommendation for a Medal of Honor for six victories in a single combat, which, after all, was a record unequaled up to that time by any aviator of any nation in the whole history of air warfare. Those six victories ran Kearby's total to fourteen, only three behind the leader—Captain Richard I. Bong.

On the twenty-ninth, Dick widened the gap again when

Colonel Paul Wurtsmith presents Bong with the Distinguished Service Cross in New Guinea. PHOTO, BONG FAMILY COLLECTION

he knocked down two Jap fighters during a big attack on Rabaul, and on November 5, when we repeated the Rabaul operation, Bong got two more enemy fighters, bringing his total up to twenty-one. I was in Brisbane when I heard about the last pair of victories. I immediately sent a message to New Guinea ordering him to report to me at once. I had promised him that hunting trip back home, and I meant to keep my promise.

He showed up the following afternoon wearing a battered cap and the regular olive-drab shirt and slacks that were the standard uniform in New Guinea. I asked him if he was ready to go home. When he happily said he was, I asked him where his clothes were. He couldn't go home in those clothes. He had to have a good-looking uniform with all his ribbons on it, and he certainly would have to get another cap. He replied that this was the only cap he owned and that his only good uniform had been lost in one of the many moves his squadron had made.

I sent him down to a good Australian tailor to get him fitted out and got all the ribbons he was entitled to sewed on. There were three rows of them, headed by the Distinguished Service Cross. When we had him completely outfitted, he still looked like a blond, blue-eyed cherub, but the uniform and the ribbons indicated that Uncle Sam had certainly gotten dividends on what it had cost to train his top-ranking fighter pilot. I then had to tell him what each ribbon stood for. He didn't particularly care but thought he ought to know in case someone back home should ask him. He left for the United States November 9, 1943, with orders to report to General Arnold in Washington and deliver a letter in which I asked Hap to let the kid go home, do some hunting, strut his stuff around the home town, and get some of his mother's cooking that he was always bragging about. I told him to be back in New Guinea by the first of February 1944.

CHAPTER 5

Bong's First Trip Home

D ICK REPORTED TO G ENERAL A RNOLD in Washington a week later, talked about the war for an hour or so, posed for innumerable pictures, and as Arnold's guest went to lunch in the dining room frequented normally only by generals, secretaries of war, and other very important people. More discussions of the war and more questions followed, which Bong answered in between bites. He always was pretty good with a knife and fork, and this food was a lot better than the canned meat, powdered eggs, and dehydrated potatoes that he had been living on for the past year. It wasn't until the end of the meal that Dick suddenly remembered the letter I had given him to deliver to Hap. He shyly pulled it out of his pocket and handed it to the general.

"General Kenney said for me to be sure to give you this letter."

Hap read it, smiled, and said, "General Kenney wants me to let you go home for a couple of months to rest up and get in some hunting. It's O.K. I'll issue the orders.

When do you want to go?"

Bong looked out the window. It was snowing, and the ceiling was practically down on the ground.

"Would it be all right if I took the train to Chicago tonight?" he asked.

Hap swallowed a couple of times and nodded. "I'll have the orders issued right away," he said. The assembled secretaries, assistant secretaries, and generals all laughed. Hap scowled and then joined them. "it's all right son, go home, get that buck, and have fun." He noticed that Bong seemed to be anxious to get started, so he got up from the table, put his arm around Dick's shoulder, and said, "Come on, Captain, let's go find out when that train leaves, and then you'd better call home and tell them when you are arriving."

At 1 A.M. on November 17, the family reunion took place. Dick's father, his mother, two brothers, and five sisters, beaming with pride, greeted him with open arms. There were a few tears, lots of smiles, and a million questions, but when Dick mentioned that he hadn't gotten much sleep on the trip from Washington, his mother interfered. "Dick, go upstairs and go to bed. You look tired. The rest of you leave him alone. He's going to be here for a couple of months, and there is plenty of time to talk to him later on."

He slept for an hour or so and then went out to call on some of his old cronies. He knew where to find them. They would all be over at the Poplar Hardware Store discussing

George Renquist, Marvin Peterson, Dick, and Earl Nevin at Grymala's restaurant/grocery store, 1943. PHOTO, BONG FAMILY COLLECTION

the hunting season, which opened the next day. There was Marvin Peterson who was acting as manager of the store as the regular manager, Robert Lundberg, was in the Army. Marvin was always a close friend of the whole Bong family and quite attentive to Dick's sister Jerry. Earl Nevin, Ludwig Maki, and Eric Le Mone were there, too, and as the word got around, newspapermen, photographers, and other old friends and neighbors came in to see their hero and welcome him home.

The first question everyone asked was how he got all those Japanese planes. Dick's answer cleared that one up with no more details than had appeared in his first combat report nearly a year before. "Oh, I'm just lucky, I guess. A lot of

Nips happened to get in my way. I keep shooting plenty of lead and finally some of them get hit."

The next question was what he was going to do while home on leave. The answer again was simple, even basic.

"I want to eat a lot of my mom's cooking and drink lots of milk. That powdered stuff we get out in

"You ought to taste my mom's cooking."
PHOTO, UNITED PRESS INTERNATIONAL

New Guinea isn't fit to drink. And powdered dehydrated potatoes—have you ever tasted them? And eggs—they are powdered too. Oh, and another thing, I want a nice big double-rich chocolate malted. I haven't seen one for more than a year. Then I'm going to do some hunting."

He posed for a few pictures but obviously didn't want to be bothered by newspapermen asking questions about the war. They didn't know anything about flying, and furthermore, he didn't like the stories that referred to him as a "killer" and his victories as "kills." When the Japs started shooting at

Hunting with his father, Carl, November, 1943.
PHOTO, UNITED PRESS INTERNATIONAL

our airmen hanging helplessly in their parachutes, on the way down from bailing out of a burning airplane, many of our pilots retaliated by doing to same thing to the Japs. Bong

Dick helps out at the family farm. PHOTO, BONG FAMILY COLLECTION

never did. Even the constant and authentic stories of atrocities committed against our aviators captured by the Japanese didn't enrage him as they did other people. He just didn't hate, and that was that. "Sure I let him go," he would say when asked why he hadn't shot at a Jap that had parachuted from a burning plane. "I figured he is in plenty of trouble already, landing in this jungle country. If he doesn't break his neck or starve to death, when he gets back to his gang, maybe he'll scare them all to death telling them what good shots we are."

Up to this time, girls had just been people as far as Dick was concerned. He had nothing against them, but the idea of settling down with one of them hadn't yet intruded in his list of things he liked to do, such as flying, hunting, fishing, playing baseball, bowling, or even eating.

In the fall of 1942, while Dick was chasing Jap airplanes over New Guinea, a local girl named Marjorie Vattendahl, then nineteen and a junior, had been elected Queen of the State Teachers College football homecoming celebration in Superior. Following precedent, it was her privilege to crown her successor the following November. It was also customary to crown a homecoming "king," but there were few male students at the college in 1943. Most were in the service or working at the Globe Shipyards in Superior. Accordingly it was decided to crown one of the air cadets in training on the campus. Then someone heard that Captain Richard Bong, the ranking American air ace and former student at State Teachers, was home on leave. Five of the girls, including Marge, rushed to the Bong home to tell him they wanted him to help Marge crown the king and queen. Dick was off hunting but due back that evening. They left their message with his sister Geraldine, then eighteen. The next day Geraldine told them that she had delivered the message and that her brother had said he "guessed he'd do the job."

The big night came. Dick crowned the king, but Marge was so awestruck gazing at the good-looking lad with the glamour of the uniform and its rows of ribbons that she forgot what she was supposed to do next. As she stood there, as if frozen, Dick smiled, took her queen's crown and placed it on the head of the new queen who was standing there so fascinated by the hero that she, too, seemed to have forgotten about the ceremony she was supposed to be a part of.

All the girls crowded around asking for a dance, but Dick said, "Sorry, but I don't dance." He sat around the rest of the evening watching the jitterbugging kids, signing short-snorter bills, and talking flying with the admiring cadets who kept leaving their partners and coming around to listen to what Bong had to say.

When the party was over, Marge and her friend Margaret Flynn started walking uptown. They stopped at the favorite student sandwich shop. Dick, his sisters Geraldine and Nelda, and his best friend Marvin Peterson, were already there. Dick saw them come in, got up, and invited them to join his table. The place was crowded, with all eyes on Bong and his three rows of ribbons. Marge pointed to them and asked what each one was for. He looked puzzled for a moment, trying to remember what I had told him back in Australia. It was of no use. He had forgotten.

"I'll be darned if I know," he replied. "Someone pins these things on me from time to time and I keep on wearing them." Everyone laughed at his apparent modesty and loved him for it. He was modest, of course, but he had told the truth. Remembering which colored ribbon signified what was just too unimportant to worry about.

The next day at luncheon, his sister Geraldine came up

to Marge and said, "Marge, Dick wants to know if you will go to dinner with him tonight on a double date with Marvin and me." Marge accepted. From then on, Dick carried his own messages, and there were dates almost every evening he was home. Very few of them were double dates after that first one.

Besides the crowning ceremony at the Teachers College dance and his dates with Marge, there were other things to keep him busy. He participated in a ship launching at the Globe Shipyards, where the "welderettes" named him their "Number-One Pin-Up Boy." The shipyards sent over steel hunting knives for the hunters in the Bong family and a set of knives to Mrs. Bong, "to cut the venison that they would bring in."

The Superior Junior Chamber of Commerce contributed the shells for Dick's .300 Savage, and both the American Legion and the Veterans of Foreign Wars made him a life member. The University of Wisconsin gave him a "W" blanket. The Poplar Lutheran Church, where Dick used to sing tenor in the choir, gave a party for him, and finally he was invited to a reception at the state capitol in Madison, given by Governor Goodland in his honor and at which the governor, after paying a tribute to the Wisconsin hero, presented him with a one-hundred-dollar War Bond on behalf of the state.

At the end of January, Dick left to keep his date with

me back in New Guinea. With him he had a picture of Marge which he was going to have blown up and pasted on the side of his fuselage alongside the collection of little Jap flags, each representing a victory.

Lockheed put the "Marge" picture on this P-38 that Dick used on his War Bond tours. PHOTO, BPNG FAMILY COLLECTION

CHAPTER 6

The Race of the Aces

ON JANUARY 20,1944, A RADIO MESSAGE CAME IN from Washington stating that Colonel Neel Kearby's Congressional Medal of Honor for shooting down six Jap airplanes in a single combat had been approved. Neel happened to be in my office in Brisbane when it came in. I immediately rushed him up to General MacArthur and had the ceremony done by the Old Man himself. The general did the thing up right, and so overwhelmed Neel that he wanted to go right back to New Guinea and knock down some more Japs to prove that he was as good as MacArthur had just told him he was.

Neel, who had scored his first victory on September 4, 1943, during the operation to capture Lae, was now credited with twenty victories, just one behind Captain Dick Bong, who was due back in a few days. I told Kearby not to engage in a race with that cool little Scandinavian boy. Bong didn't care who was high man. He would never be in a race, and I didn't want Kearby to press his luck and take too many chances for the sake of having his name first on the scoreboard. I told him to be satisfied from now on to dive through a Jap formation, shoot down one airplane, head for a cloud, and come on home. In that way, as he was an excellent shot and a superb flier, he would live forever, but if he kept coming back to get the second one and the third one, he would be asking for trouble and giving the Jap top cover a good chance to knock him off. Kearby agreed that it was good advice, but said he would like to get an even fifty before he went home. When I suggested that I'd like to send him home now for a month, he said, "I've only one to go to tie Bong. If you send me home now, I'll never catch up. Let me get fifty first." I said all right, but I wished he would try to settle for one Nip per week.

Lieutenant Colonel Tommy Lynch, who had led the P-38s in their first flight over Dobodura in December 1942, had just returned and was anxious to go after the top score. Tommy had led the pack with sixteen victories when I sent him back on leave the previous fall but now he needed four to catch Kearby and five to tie Bong. I told him to take it easy, too, and not to get in a race with anybody. He left New Guinea, promising to behave himself. Bong, Kearby, and Lynch were the big three in the Southwest Pacific as February 1944 began. Major George Welch, with sixteen to his credit, had gone home in November 1943. Captain Roberts, who had knocked down fifteen Nips in eleven weeks, was killed over Finschhafen on November 9, 1943, and Major Edward Cragg, also credited

with a score of fifteen, was shot down in flames over Gloucester on December 26 of that same year.

The nearest fighter pilots to the top three now were Major
Gerald Johnson, Major Tommy McGuire's, and Captain James
Watkins, all crack shots, who were getting Japs at the rate of
two or three in a combat and were in a triple tie at eleven.

By the middle of February, when Bong got back to
New Guinea, Lynch had run his score up to eighteen. On
Bong's arrival, General "Squeeze" Wurtsmith, the head of
the Fifth Fighter Command, assigned Tommy to his staff
as his operative officer and Dick as Lynch's assistant When
they wanted to know if that meant they were out of combat,
Wurtsmith said that while they were no longer assigned to a
combat squadron, they could "free lance" together as a team,
either alone or attaching themselves to any squadron in the
command, whenever they could be spared from their staff
duties. "Squeeze" ran the Fighter Command without too
much help, so they figured they would get enough action so
that they wouldn't forget how to fly.

In the late afternoon of February 27, we picked up and
decoded a Jap radio message which gave the time of arrival at
the Wewak airdrome of a Jap transport plane carrying some
staff officers from Rabaul. By the time we got the information, it was almost too late for an interception, but we gave
the information to Bong and Lynch, who hurriedly took off
and flew wide open all the way arriving over Wewak about

two minutes before the Jap plane was scheduled to land. The inconsiderate Nip, however, was ahead of schedule, had already landed, and was taxiing down the runway. Lynch dived to the attack but found that in his hurry to get away, his gun sights had not been installed. He called to Bong to take the Jap. Bong fired one burst—the plane was enveloped in flames for a second or two, and then it blew up. No one was seen to leave it, before or after the attack. The two kids then machine-gunned a party of at least a hundred Japs who had evidently come down to greet the visitors. Subsequent frantic radio messages passing between Wewak and Tokyo indicated that the victims were a major general, a brigadier, and a whole staff of high-ranking officers.

On their return, Bong and Lynch came over to my New Guinea advanced headquarters and told me the story. I wanted to let Bong have credit for an airplane destroyed in combat, but of course it was on the ground, so it couldn't count on the victory scoreboard. We counted only wing shots in the Southwest Pacific. I asked Dick if he was sure that the Jap transport was actually on the ground when he hit it. Couldn't it have been just an inch or so above the runway? Maybe the plane's wheels had touched and it had bounced back into the air temporarily? Everyone knew that some Japs were poor pilots. Lynch stood there grinning, and said that whatever Bong decided was okay with him. Dick listened seriously, as if it were a problem in mathematics, and then looked up and said simply, earnestly, and without a trace of disappointment, "General, he was on the ground all right. He had even stopped rolling."

Everyone was now watching the scores of these two and Neel Kearby. A few days after Bong's return from his leave in the United States, Kearby had shot down two Jap fighters, bringing the score up to twenty-two. Neel felt pretty good until he landed back at his home airdrome where he was greeted with the news that Bong had shot down a Jap fighter that morning over New Britain. The score was now tied, but it was at twenty-two. A few days later, each of the three leaders added another victory. With Neel and Dick each at twenty-three and Lynch with nineteen, Eddie Rickenbacker's old World War I record of twenty-six didn't look so far away now.

On March 4, Kearby decided to break the tie. With his group headquarters flight, of Major Sam Blair and Captains Dunham and Banks, Neel headed for the Wewak area and trouble. Just west of the village of Dagua, sighting a formation of fifteen Jap aircraft, he signaled for the attack. A quick burst, and a Nip plane went spinning to the earth in flames. One ahead. Now for a little velvet for that lead position. Neel turned back into the Jap formation and, with a beautiful long-range shot from a sixty-degree angle from the rear, got his second victim with a single burst. As he pulled away, three Jap fighters closed in from above and behind. Dunham got one. Banks got another. The third Jap poured a burst into Neel's cockpit from close range. The P-47 with twenty-three Jap flags painted on its side plunged straight down. It never came out of the dive, and no parachute opened, as it kept going until it disappeared into the jungle bordering on the Jap airdrome at Dagua.

Somehow I felt a little glad that Neel never knew that Dick Bong had added two more to his score that morning, shooting down a couple of Jap bombers during a fighter sweep over Tadji, New Guinea. Lynch, in that same flight, had bagged a bomber and a fighter, bringing his total up to twenty-one.

On March 9, Bong and Lynch flew another mission over the Tadji area to see whether or not the Japs were filling up the hole in the airdrome, which we had bombed heavily a few days before. They couldn't find any airplanes to shoot at in the air or on the ground, so looking for some kind of target, they spied Jap luggers just offshore, heading west toward Hollandia. Burst after burst of the .50-caliber guns of each plane poured into the Jap vessels, which responded with their own deck defense guns. Suddenly Bong saw Lynch pull around and head for shore. One of his engines was smoking. Then, just as he got to the shore line, Dick saw in quick succession a propeller flying off, Tommy taking to his parachute, and at almost the same instant, the plane exploding. Bong flew around for several minutes to see if he could discover any indication that by some miracle Tommy had survived. There wasn't a chance, and Dick knew it. The chute had burned up with the explosion, and probably Lynch was dead before his body hit the ground.

Dick flew back and reported. I was afraid that seeing Tommy go might affect his nerve, so I ordered him to Brisbane to ferry a new airplane back to his squadron and sent a message to the depot commander there that if the airplane was ready to fly before another couple of weeks, I would demote him at least two grades.

It turned out that I needn't have worried about Bong's morale. I came back to Brisbane after he had been there about ten days, eating a lot of good food, drinking gallons of fresh milk, and sleeping at least ten hours out of every twenty-four. He had begun to get bored with going out to the depot each day and being told that his airplane was not yet ready. For the past couple of days he had been working with a sergeant out there, designing and building an attachment to carry a couple cases of Coca-Cola on each wing when he ferried the airplane back to New Guinea. He then collected his four cases of Coke and loaded them ready to go. A little later, he showed up at my headquarters and asked where he could get coupons to buy sheets, which were rationed articles. We asked him if he wanted them for his whole outfit, but no, he just wanted four for himself. We gave him his coupons and sent a major on the staff who knew where to buy sheets along with Dick. With the Coke and the sheets, he now figured the trip to Australia was really worth while. I took him up to General MacArthur's office for a visit. He was so impressed that he walked around as if in a daze for the rest of the day. I held him for two more days to let him recover and then told the depot commander to let Dick have the airplane. Just before he took off, I told him to fight the Japs in the air from now on and leave the strafing jobs to someone else. Besides, the liquid cooling system of the P-38 was too vulnerable. Strafing against anyone who shot back should be done by a plane with an air-cooled engine.

On April 3, he got in a fight over Hollandia while with his old Ninth Squadron, escorting a big bombing raid on the Jap airdromes there. A Jap fighter got into an argument with Dick and lost. Number twenty-five.

On April 12, we again raided Hollandia with one hundred and eighty-eight bombers and sixty-seven fighters. Twenty Jap fighters intercepted. Our P-38s shot down eight of them and listed another as probable. Two of the Nip planes that were definitely destroyed in combat were added to the score of Captain Richard I. Bong, making his score twenty-seven, one more than the record set by Eddie Rickenbacker in France in World War I. The one listed as probable was also one of Bong's victims. He told me that the Jap plane he had reported as a "probable" in the combat of April 12, near Hollandia, had gone into the water in Tannemerah Bay about twenty miles west of Hollandia. The reason it had been called a probable was that no one except Bong had seen it go down, and his camera gun was not installed that day. Under the rules, he could not get credit for it unless the victory was confirmed by an eyewitness, or the wreckage of the Jap plane was found where he claimed it had crashed. He showed me on the photograph of the area exactly where the plane went

Dick Bong in the cockpit of his P-38 bearing flags denoting the 27 Japanese planes he has shot down. PHOTO, INTERNATIONAL SOUNDPHOTO

into the water and said that it was a single-seater fighter of the type we called an Oscar, that he had hit the left wing, the pilot, and the engine, but that the plane had not burned.

When we captured the Hollandia area a couple of weeks later, I got a diver to go down where Dick had said the airplane went in. The diver located it almost instantly, and we pulled it up. It was an Oscar. The left wing had eleven bullet holes in it, the pilot had been hit in the head and neck, two cylinder engines were knocked out, and there was no sign of fire. I put out an order giving Bong official credit for the victory—his twenty-eighth.

A couple of days later, a radio came in from General Arnold—at least it was signed with his name. Later on I found that one of his staff had written and sent it without telling Hap about it. It read:

> Concern is expressed over the high loss rate of fighter pilots who have shot down many enemy aircraft. Your comments are requested concerning the desirability of restricting from action combat flying or return to United States of this type of personnel. A case in point is Captain Bong, who is credited with twenty-seven enemy aircraft. Only very recently we have lost the invaluable services of Colonels Kearby and Lynch.
>
> —ARNOLD

Although he had been back only two and half months since his last trip home, the Pentagon seemed so worried about him that while I didn't agree with their thinking in the matter, I decided that I would use Arnold's message as an excuse to send Dick home, let him see his girl back in Poplar, Wisconsin, and be acclaimed as America's leading air ace of any war. He had mentioned a gunnery course.

I wired Hap that I was taking Bong out of combat to run a gunnery course for the Fighter Command but that I believed he ought to get the very latest information in the United States. Accordingly, I asked that after two or three weeks' leave at home Dick take the aerial gunnery course and then come back to me. I would then have him instruct the rest of my fighter pilots.

After all, the race of the aces was over, at least for the time being. The nearest score to Bong's twenty-seven was Major Tommy McGuire's twenty.

CHAPTER 7

Rickenbacker and I
Keep a Promise

As soon as the news came in about Dick's combat over Hollandia, I ordered him to report to me at my headquarters in Brisbane and told my personnel officer to make Bong a major, with rank to date from April 12, 1944. I then sent a message to General Arnold giving him Dick's latest score, with a copy to Eddie Rickenbacker. The next day Eddie wired me that he was sending me a special-delivery letter that he wanted me to deliver. His message to Bong read:

> Just received the good news that you are the first one to break my record in World War I by bringing down twenty-seven planes in combat as well as your promotion so justly deserved. I hasten to offer my sincere congratulations, with the hope that you will double or treble this number. But in trying, use the same cool, calculating technique that has brought you results to date, for we will need your kind back home after this war is over. My promise of a case of scotch still holds good. So be on the lookout for it.

General Arnold sent Dick two cases of "pop" with the message:

> I understand that you prefer this type of refreshment to others. You thoroughly deserve to have the kind you want. The Army Air Forces are proud of you and your splendid record. Congratulations.

Eddie Rickenbacker had mentioned to newspapermen around Washington that he had promised a case of scotch to the one who first broke his World War I record and that he hoped he wouldn't have too much trouble getting hold of a case. The story hit the headlines of newspapers all over the country along with the story of Bong's achievement. Inside of forty-eight hours, Eddie received around fifty offers of scotch whisky. The first one came in from a nightclub proprietor in Nogales, Mexico, named Demetrio Kyriakis, who said he wanted to send it, "on behalf of the people of Nogales." A woman liquor dealer wired Eddie, "I've been saving a case for a very special occasion—and this is it."

When Bong reported to me in Brisbane, I told him that in a week or so I was going to send him back to the United States to take a course in aerial gunnery that he had talked to me about. It was a funny thing, but he was not a good shot. He got his Nips because he was good enough as an aviator to place himself within a few yards of the enemy plane so that he couldn't miss. If Dick once got on a Jap's tail, he stayed there and closed in, no matter what maneuver his opponent made. On the other hand, whenever he tried a long-range shot, he missed. He had said many times that he wished he could take a good gunnery course. I figured that now was the time to get it in. Also, while he was back in the United States, he could see that girl whose picture was on the fuselage of his P-38 alongside a collection of twenty-five little Jap flags. I told him he would not go back into combat until I said he could, so to stay around Brisbane for a few days and enjoy himself before I sent him home.

Dick was quite happy about the prospects of another trip back home, but he wanted to know if I would let him go back into combat when he returned. I told him that I would think about it but I might need him on another job first. Then he wanted to know what was going to happen to his airplane while he was away. He knew I was short of P-38s but . . . I removed his last worry by telling him that the airplane would be kept in a depot in Port Moresby ready to fly the day he got back and that no one else would fly it until then.

About a week later Eddie Rickenbacker's case of scotch arrived aboard an air transport plane. I added mine, a case of champagne, and two cases of Coca-Cola, and sent Dick up to New Guinea with the whole works, to give a party for anyone he wanted to invite, and then report back to me.

Dick asked all the pilots in the Fifth Fighter Command

and some of his friends in the bomber outfits to help him get rid of his cargo. Everyone had fun, but there were so many customers they were lucky to get one drink apiece.

The next day Bong and Eddie Rickenbacker had a two-way radio telephone conversation that was arranged and broadcast by NBC. Dick thought it would be fun when he was told about it, but when the time came for him to talk he was as nervous as a stage-struck actor on opening night.

Here is part of the conversation as recorded:

EDDIE: "How does it feel to be top man?"

BONG: "Thanks for those kind words, Captain Rickenbacker, but you know every flier over here is trying to knock down as many Japs as possible."

EDDIE: "Tell me Major Bong, what quality of Jap fighter pilot are you meeting now?"

BONG: "The pilots out here—I don't think they are nearly as good as they used to be. The old-timers had more experience. The present ones seem easier to get. It's not only that, Captain Rickenbacker, our planes and fliers are better than the Japs too."

The broadcast offered nothing startling, but in time of war there are censors who are inherently opposed to letting human-interest stories get out. I would like to have heard something about those cases of scotch and what happened to them, but it didn't get into the conversation. It was probably just as well. The country was supposed to realize that we were at war instead of thinking about a lot of fighter pilots relaxing over a drink of scotch.

Dick left for the United States on May 3, armed with another letter to General Hap Arnold, which read:

Headquarters
Far East Air Forces
3rd May 1944

Dear General Arnold:

This note is being delivered to you by your top-scoring fighter pilot, Major Richard I. Bong. If consistent with your procedures in cases of this kind, I would like to have Bong given about thirty days' leave followed by about the same period collecting all the latest information on aerial gunnery and fighter tactics. At the conclusion of this tour of instruction, I want him back here to take charge of gunnery training at Nadzab, where I am establishing an advanced combat training center for both the Fifth and the Thirteenth Air Forces. In this way I hope to have Bong's knowledge and technique imparted to all the incoming fighter pilots. I have sold Bong the idea that if he can impart his technique to ten other youngsters who will thereby be able to shoot down ten Nips apiece, he will be directly or indirectly responsible for more air victories than if he tried to do the whole thing himself. Bong, of course, is extremely anxious to return to combat but I have told him that this is very unlikely, as no matter how much flying and gunnery he does in training, I am afraid he will get a little bit rusty for combat.

The main reason for my writing this note is that I am afraid there will be a natural desire to keep Bong in the United States. He himself is very anxious to return to the theater and I believe he will be of most value here in the job to which I have assigned him. If you feel that some additional time for publicity purposes or War Bond campaigns is definitely worth while, I have no objection, but I would like to see him back here by August 1 at the latest.

Sincerely,
George C. Kenney
Lieutenant General U.S.A.
Commander

A totally unexpected development followed Eddie Rick-enbacker and my offer to contribute to a celebration of setting a new score of air victories. It then started interfering with the war effort by taking valuable time to reply to a flood of messages of criticism. I knew it was a year of campaigning for the election of a new president and a lot of new congressmen and that possibly that was why the messages were deemed important enough to answer, but to me it was the question of dignifying the outburst of a lot of crackpots. Rickenbacker and I were accused of seducing our pilots with liquor to carry out their missions and bribing American youth with booze to be patriotic. Individuals and some prohibition societies took part in the protest. My own impulse was to ignore the whole thing, but after all, we were still in a war that was by no means settled. The stereotyped answer became, that the whole story was silly, as Major Bong did not drink, and to help him celebrate his victory with his associates, both General MacArthur and I had sent him cases of soft drinks. Eddie told me that he, too, had lots of mail on the subject, most of it disapproving of his role in the story. With the whole world on fire, to me it really was another instance of "much ado, about nothing."

CHAPTER 8

Bong's Second Trip Home

MAJOR RICHARD I. BONG, TOP AMERICAN ACE of World Wars I and II, arrived in Washington on May 9, 1944. This time he remembered to give my letter to General Arnold as soon as he was ushered into the office of the Army Air Forces Commander. Hap already knew the contents as I had wired him the whole story a few days before. He looked over the letter and told Dick that he was going to give him three weeks at home on leave and that about the middle of August he would be going to the gunnery school at Matagora, Texas, for the course, which would take about three weeks. In the meantime, to help out the war effort, he wanted Dick to have some press conferences, visit a few places around the country, and let people know that the Air Force was playing a part in the war.

Bong's first press conference was held on May 11 at the Pentagon. Newspapermen and public relations people who were there still remember it. Dick was not a public relations officer's delight. He had to submit to the interview and was rather bored by the whole business, and he didn't care at all for the attempts to "brief" him on what he should say, before the questioning started. In response to some questions about the capabilities of our pilots as compared to the Japs, Bong answered that he thought that the average American made a better pilot than the average Jap, but that we were not giving enough training to our men and were not paying enough attention to gunnery. Dick went into quite a bit of detail while the public relations colonel accompanying him squirmed in agony at such sacrilege. Finally he could stand it no longer. He interrupted, and a little apologetically submitted an alternate version which was what he thought Bong really intended to convey. "I think that about covers what you meant, doesn't it, Major Bong?" he concluded. Dick yawned and said. "Oh, I guess that's as good as anything if that's what you want." The press laughed, the colonel turned red, and the conference was over. There were the usual pictures, but the only other information that the newspapermen got out of him was what he wanted to do after the war.

Dick's answer was, "I want to keep on flying. I'll never give it up as long as I am physically fit. I'd like to have a cottage on Lake Gordon with a big fireplace—and a hangar."

Eddie Rickenbacker dropped around that afternoon to chat. The two aviators had trouble trying to talk flying without a lot of people standing around bothering them. They finally wound up outside the Pentagon, sitting on

Curbstone session with Eddie Rickenbacker. PHOTO, WIDE WORLD PHOTOS

the steps, having a grand time comparing the tactics of flying a World War I Spad, at 120 miles an hour, with the P-38 of World War II at more than four hundred. They both agreed that gunnery and gunnery sights still needed improving, as in both wars it was necessary to get in close to your opponent if you expected to get hits. Dick mentioned that it was almost essential to shoot down the Jap aviator to prevent him from ramming you. Eddie laughed and said, "I'm sure glad the Germans didn't try that stuff on us back in 1918." Eddie asked him what he was going to do after he finished the gunnery course. "Oh, I'm going back to the Southwest Pacific," said Bong. "General Kenney wants me back for some job. I hope he doesn't stop me from flying combat though. I believe I'd go nuts if I couldn't get back into combat."

The next morning, Dick visited the Senate and was recognized by Senator Robert M. La Follette, Jr., of Wisconsin, who pointed to him seated in the gallery and then made a ten-minute speech praising the young hero from his home state. The senators gave him a standing ovation. This was followed by a lunch with Senators La Follette, Barkley of Kentucky, White and Brewster of Maine, Connally of Texas, George and Russell of Georgia, Vandenburg of Michigan, Taft of Ohio, Gurney of South Dakota, Hill of Alabama, and Reynolds of North Carolina.

They were all very nice to him, praised him, congratulated him, and in general, showed him a good time. His reticence, which they took for the becoming modesty of a hero, charmed them, but as soon as he could, he excused himself, to get back to the Pentagon where he could find some aviators to talk to.

That evening he took the train for Pittsburgh where he paid a call on Mrs. Rosemary Lynch, the widow of Lieutenant Colonel Thomas J. Lynch, who had been killed on March 6 near Tadji, in Dutch New Guinea. He had a few snapshots of Tommy that he gave Rosemary before he left for Chicago on his way home.

On May 14, he arrived in Chicago, where he was met by his father and mother and his girl, Marjorie Vattendahl.

Marjorie, then twenty, was a senior at Superior State Teachers College but she had taken a couple of days' leave to greet the lad whose airplane carried her picture. The trip from Chicago to Poplar was made by automobile. There were lots of questions and answers about the war and about happenings in Poplar with plans for his three weeks' leave, but Dick still managed to doze for a couple of hours before they reached home that evening.

In Poplar, for the next few days, Dick found that he was

Main street hero. PHOTO, UNITED PRESS INTERNATIONAL

still a celebrity. The local papers wanted interviews. Chicago, Milwaukee, and Minneapolis sent newspapermen and photographers, and the wire services helped in keeping Bong and the whole family occupied. Everyone wanted to know if Dick and Marjorie were engaged and when they were going to get married. They agreed that they were engaged but there would be no marriage as long as Dick remained in combat.

When his mother was asked if she didn't worry about her son fighting in the Pacific, she replied, "I quit worrying about him a long time ago. The only time he ever had an

Family scene with Marge.
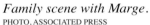
PHOTO, ASSOCIATED PRESS

Marge's "piggyback" flight. PHOTO, LOCKHEED

accident was when he fell from a swing when he was a school-boy and broke his arm."

During one of the interviews, someone mentioned that the radio had just sent out an item stating that Bong had been given credit for his twenty-eighth victory. A previous "probable" had been confirmed. Dick's comment was, "Yes, I was sure I got him. He was pretty good at acrobatics but not so hot as a combat pilot. I got him separated from the rest of his gang and chased him out over the water. I kept pouring lead at him, and I guess he must have run into some of the bullets, for he crashed into the bay."

The remainder of his leave passed fairly quietly. He did manage to get hold of a P-38 at a nearby Air Force field one

To Major Bong
Such a job really
Best Wishes
Barbara Stanwyck

To Major Bong
With every
good wishes
and sincere
congratulations
Jack Benny

day and put on an exhibition of acrobatics and low-altitude buzzing of his home town that the people of Poplar still talk about, but eating, sleeping, visiting with his old friends, and dating Marjorie pretty well filled up his schedule.

A few days before his leave was up, he heard that a Mrs. Stanley Johnson, the widow of one of his wingmen who had been shot down over Rabaul about four months before, was visiting Superior. Dick immediately drove over to call on her and spent the whole afternoon talking with her about her husband, what a grand flier and gentleman he had been and how proud he was to have flown with him. "By protecting my tail, he made it possible for me to shoot down a lot of Japs. He should have had the credit for them—not me," said Dick.

About the first of June, he reported back to General Arnold, who put him on tour, visiting training fields all over the country, talking to youngsters getting ready for combat about what was going on and how the air war was being fought out in the Pacific.

He told me afterward that he visited so many places and gave the same "pep" talk so many times that he had lost count. He hoped he would never get a job like that again. Almost everywhere he went, people recognized him and crowded around to talk to him, get his autograph, and ask

Dick posed for hundreds of pictures; (clockwise from top left) with celebrities Angela Lansbury (and Marge), Judy Garland, Jack Benny, and Barbara Stanwyck. PHOTOS, BONG FAMILY COLLECTION

him to pose for snapshots. He said that he had heard and answered the same questions so often that he could do it in his sleep. He posed for hundreds of pictures, but although he was always good-natured about it, he got rather bored when so many people wanted to have their pictures taken talking with him, shaking his hand, or with an arm around his shoulder. Frankly, he didn't care much for the hero role, except perhaps a little back home at the Poplar Hardware Store with his old friends and neighbors around him.

The one place he remembered most favorably was Wilmington, North Carolina. He landed at Blumenthal Field, just outside of town, late one afternoon. After dinner he went into town and wandered around alone, looking in the store windows, and finally stopped in a drugstore to get a double- rich chocolate malted milk-shake. No one recognized him, and Dick was so happy about not being bothered that he hung around town until the stores closed before he went back to the field.

The next morning the press interviewed him. What was the purpose of his visit? "I have to talk to the troops at the base about the war—by order of the Chief of the Air Force," said Bong. What was he going to do after the war? "Be a farmer, I guess," replied Dick. They did the best they could with their stories but they couldn't get much material out of Bong to build on. Whenever there was an Air Force public relations officer around, Dick would point to him and say, "Well, that's enough from me. I haven't anything more. Ask him the questions. He has all the latest dope."

One of his assignments took him to Los Angeles. Some of the youngsters at one of the training fields near there observed that Bong was quite obviously bored and invited him to go to the big city, have dinner, listen to the music, and perhaps see some entertainment. Dick thought it was a good idea.

As they entered the night spot and were standing there waiting to be shown to a table, a gorgeous little blonde broke away from a group at the bar, rushed up to Bong, threw her arms around him, and cried, "Oh, Dick darling, it's so good to see you again."

Dick disengaged himself, looked at her, puzzled for a moment, and said, "I'm sorry, Miss, but you must think I'm someone else."

"Why, Dick," she replied, "surely you remember those days back home when we used to go out to the club on Lake Wabanaka and dance every Saturday night. Those were grand times, weren't they, Dick?" "Lady," said Dick solemnly, "you must be mistaken. There isn't any clubhouse on Lake Wabanaka—in fact I don't know any lake in Wisconsin by that name, and besides, I don't dance."

The girl turned on her heel and, quite evidently vastly annoyed, went back to the bar, picked up a wrap that she had left on a chair, and left. Dick looked after her as though still puzzled. The gang with him was not so polite. They all laughed.

However, Bong had a good time for the rest of the evening. The food was good and the floor show was entertaining.

On one of his trips to Washington to get a new set of instructions for another tour around the country Dick ran into Major Bob Johnson, who had just come home from the European theater as the leading American air ace there. He had also scored twenty-seven victories, to top Rickenbacker's old score, but Bong had beaten him to it by about a month.

They first met in a conference room in the Pentagon on June 7. Generals, congressmen and their wives, and miscellaneous people rounded up by the public relations section were there to meet the two top Air Force aces. Through twenty minutes of introductions and greetings to Dick Bong his standardized comment to everyone was "Glad to meet you," and "It's a hell of a war, ain't it?"

When he was introduced to Johnson, he loosened up a bit. Here was a fellow flier and a good one, too. Here was someone he could talk to. Dick stared at Bob a moment, then smiled that disarming, cherubic smile of his and said, "You're a little guy, too, aren't you? I'm sure glad you got here. Maybe they are going to put you on the road, too, and help me go through all this stuff. I'd rather have a Jap Zero on my tail than go through all these dinners and speeches I've been going to."

They moved over to a corner by themselves and talked flying and about what they were going to do next. Dick said,

"I've got to do some more of this traveling and making speeches before I go to Matagorda for the gunnery course. I don't know what they'll do with me after that."

Johnson had the same type of assignment ahead of him, after a leave at home in Lawton, Oklahoma, only his gunnery course would be in Galveston, Texas.

The luncheon then began, following which they went to visit General Arnold in his office. After half-an-hour or so talking combat flying and comparing the differences between fighting the Japs and the Germans and arguing about the relative merits of the P-38 and the P-47, the single-engined fighter in which Johnson had gained all his victories, Bong left to take on another round of the steak and speaking circuit.

In August he was ordered to Matagorda on the Gulf Coast of Texas for a month of gunnery training. On completion, he headed back to the Pacific, reporting to me at my headquarters in Hollandia, Dutch New Guinea, on September 10, 1944.

CHAPTER 9

Bong as Instructor

DICK WAS QUITE ENTHUSIASTIC about the aerial-gunnery course he had just completed. He said he really had learned so much about shooting that he was ashamed of the way he had wasted ammunition in getting the twenty-eight victories he was credited with. He was all ready now to go out and prove it, if I would just give him an assignment to a fighter squadron.

I told him that I wanted him to visit all the fighter outfits and teach them what he had learned back home. I said, "Look, Dick, if I let you back into combat, I know you will knock down another twenty or thirty Nips, but if, instead, you can teach a hundred pilots to get one Jap apiece without getting themselves shot down, I'll be way ahead of the game."

He didn't look too happy about the job I'd given him but he cheered up a little when I told him that after a month of his teaching job I'd let him go along once in a while to see whether or not his pupils had absorbed their instructions. Even when I insisted that I didn't want him to do any shooting except in self-defense, he didn't seem to be too worried. I told him that while he had been gone, Colonel Charles

Lindbergh had been in the theater and had taught the pilots how to use their fuel to get a lot more range out of the P-38 than before. While he was teaching gunnery, he should learn the new stuff about saving his fuel, or he would not be able to accompany the gang all the way on some of the long trips. He went away happy. He had a job again.

Major Tommy McGuire, of the 475th Fighter Group, also equipped with P-38s, came in a few days later to see if I would overrule the doctors and let him fly again. McGuire had arrived in the Southwest Pacific Theater, back in the spring of 1943, to find that Bong had eight victories. Every time he shot down a Jap, he'd find that Bong had also gotten one. He'd always been eight behind. When Bong got up to twenty-eight and I sent him home, McGuire had just made his score twenty. He said, "Now is my chance. Dick will be away for at least three months. By the time he gets back, he'll be number two on that scoreboard."

Japs got scarce about that time, however, and just as his group moved to Hollandia and it looked as though business was about to pick up again, Tommy had a siege of dengue fever. And when he was recovering from that, malaria hit him. He had been in the hospital ever since and had just managed to get released the day before, but the medicos had stipulated that he do no flying for another ten days. His eyes were keen but he looked pretty thin to me.

"I just heard Bong is back, and I'm still eight behind,"

he mourned, "and by the time those fool docs let me fly again, there is no telling how many that guy will knock down. General, how about letting me go?"

I told him "no," and to take it easy until he was right again. I wanted to see some more meat on those bones of his so that I could be sure he had enough strength to pull a trigger. There was no need for him to worry, as I had put Bong on a gunnery instructing job that would keep him busy and out of combat for at least three weeks. As a matter of fact, I hadn't even assigned him to a combat outfit. Anyhow, no one was going to get many Nips until we got to the Philippines. There were simply no fights in the theater within the range of the P-38 any more. He was disappointed when I told him I would not overrule the doctors, but when he heard that Bong was not going back into combat for a while he cheered up. He said he guessed he'd go back to his squadron and see what had been going on since he went to the hospital.

On October 10, we pulled a big raid on the Japanese-held oil refinery at Balikpapan on the island of Borneo. One hundred and six heavy bombers were escorted by thirty-six P-38s. The Japs put ninety fighters into the air against us. They lost sixty-one of them. We lost a fighter and four bombers.

Two of the Jap planes shot down figured as numbers twenty-nine and thirty on the score of Major Richard I. Bong, who had flown up from Nadzab, where he had been instructing the newly

Bong as an insrtructor.   PHOTO, U.S. AIR FORCE

arrived pilots in gunnery, to see how his pupils were doing when they came to shooting for keeps.

I noticed in the report he turned in that the first Jap airplane had been downed at an altitude of 1,500 feet and the second at 18,000 feet. I said, "Dick, I want to talk to you about those two Japs that you shot down in self-defense. How high were you flying when you saw that first Jap plane and how high was he?"

"Well, General, I was with the rest of the fighter cover at about eighteen thousand feet when I saw this Nip plane headed west toward Balikpapan. He was pretty low, all right. I guess at about one thousand five hundred or maybe two thousand feet, but I figured he had seen our bombers and was going back to warn the rest of his gang and I'd better stop him. I don't believe he even saw me coming."

"That doesn't sound much like self defense to me," I said, "but how about the second one?"

"Oh, that really was self-defense," Bong insisted. "Honest, when I climbed back to join the rest of our fighters, the fight was on, and this bird tried to make a pass at me. I had to shoot him down or he might have gotten me."

He then tried to change the subject. "General, that gunnery course I took back home is really good. All the outfit did much better today than ever before. They didn't fire anywhere near as much ammunition as they generally do, and they got a lot of Nips."

"How many rounds did you fire, and how far away did you start shooting?" I asked. I pretended that I didn't know he had switched the subject on me. After all, how mad could I get at a guy who had just shot down two enemy aircraft and brought his own plane back without a scratch on it?

"Well, I know it is a good course, " Dick replied, "and the next time I'm going to try some long-range shooting, but today, just to make sure, each time I pushed the gun barrels into the Nip's cockpit and pulled the trigger. I only fired two bursts, one for each Jap."

I told him to keep on with his instructing job but for heaven's sake to watch his step. He was doing too good a job bringing up the scores of the rest of the fighter boys to take any chances of depriving me of an instructor. He left, solemnly promising that he would be careful.

That evening I wired General Arnold:

During the strike on Balikpapan by five heavy-bomber groups on October 10th, Major Richard Bong in a P-38 accompanied the escorting fighters to observe the results of the gunnery instruction he had been giving since his return from the United States. While conducting his observations, he was forced in self-defense to shoot down two Nip aircraft. While regrettable, this brings his official score to thirty enemy aircraft destroyed in aerial combat. Have cautioned Bong to be more careful in the future.

Hap replied: "Congratulations to Major Bong on his continued mastery of the manly art of self-defense. Feel sure your warning will have desired effect."

Major Tommy McGuire finally got out of the clutches of the doctors in time to make this raid. Two Japs tried to argue the question of air superiority with Tommy. They lost. That brought McGuire's score up to twenty-two—still eight behind Dick Bong.

On October 20, 1944, our troops landed at Tacloban and Dulag, two towns on Leyte Gulf on the east coast of Leyte Island in the Philippines. Near both places were old Jap airdromes that we went to work on immediately so that I could move my fighters and bombers forward to support our operations to reoccupy the Philippines. Both airdromes were in bad shape from bombing attacks and were too small anyway for our aircraft. Until they were ready for occupancy, the aircraft carriers of Admiral Kinkade's Seventh Fleet would support our ground forces and provide cover for the shipping in Leyte Gulf.

For the next week the Jap aviators made our lives miserable. Several times each day and every night they raided our shipping in the Gulf and took pot shots at our engineers trying to get the airdromes in shape. Their aim was not too good, but they did interfere with the work. On the twenty-fifth, a big Jap fleet steamed east through the San Bernardino Straits and before they were driven back had sunk a couple of Kinkade's flattops and damaged several others. All those still afloat had to withdraw for refueling, repairs, restocking of bombs and ammunition, and resting the crews.

We worked all that night on the Tacloban strip, in spite of a couple of bombing attacks, and mobilized all the manpower we could get hold of the next day. Engineers, airmen, Filipino civilians, and even some Chinese worked like beavers laying steel mat in place as fast as it could be unloaded from the supply vessels. By evening we had a 1,500-foot runway and the surface prepared to lay an additional 2,000 feet of mat. It would be a little close, but a good P-38 pilot could land that short. I figured that by noon the next day we would have a landing strip about three thousand feet long so I wired General Whitehead that we had room for 34 P-38s at Tacloban and to have that number come up from our advanced field on Morotai Island to land at noon on October 27. I also said in the message that I wanted nothing but experts on short landing in this first contingent.

About ten minutes before noon, General MacArthur and I were at the table having lunch at his headquarters in Tacloban. Suddenly we heard a low drone of engines. The general said, "Hello George, what's that?" I said, "That's my P-38s from the Forty-ninth Fighter Group," and got up from the table. MacArthur was already ahead of me and called for me to get into his car. We drove out to the field. All over the area you could hear soldiers and Filipinos yelling and cheering at the sight of those P-38s. They looked good to me, too, as the whole thirty-four of them came in low over our heads, flying a formation that would have been a credit to the Air Force at an inaugural parade back home.

The kids landed, taxied into position, and as they got out, I introduced them to General MacArthur, who shook hands all around and patted them on the back. These were the old-timers, the veterans of the Forty-ninth Group, which to date was credited with nearly five hundred victories. General MacArthur knew many of them and had followed their careers since they first got into action two and a half years before. They all liked the general, too, and got a great kick out of having him meet them, particularly when he said, "You don't know how glad I am to see you."

The last plane to land taxied out to the end of the line opposite where I was standing with General MacArthur talking to the gang. A short, stocky, towheaded lad eased himself out of the cockpit and started back behind the tail of the airplane.

I yelled, "Bong, come over here." The kid came over and saluted, looking at me solemnly, and then grinned shyly as he saw MacArthur standing there smiling at him.

"Who told you to come up here?" I demanded.

"Oh, I had permission from General Whitehead," he answered.

"Did he tell you that you could fly combat after you got here?" I asked.

"No," replied the cherub, "but can I?"

Everybody laughed now, including me. I told him that we were in such a fix that anyone could fly combat who knew anything about a P-38 and had one to fly.

Bong saluted happily and went back to his airplane to get it gassed up and ready to go.

About five o'clock that afternoon, five Jap fighter planes came over on a raid. We had just installed a radar, and while it wasn't working very well yet, we could get about ten minutes' warning of an attack.

Lieutenant Colonel Walker, the group commander, Lieutenant Colonel Bob Morrisey who had shot down the first Jap plane for the Forty-ninth Fighter Group back in March 1942 and was still in there pitching, Lieutenant Colonel Gerald Johnson, the group executive officer, and Dick Bong took off to intercept. Walker had engine trouble right after the take-off and came back mad as a wet hen. The other three did their stuff. Johnson got two of the Nips and Morrisey and Bong racked up one apiece. The remaining Jap disappeared in the clouds and got away.

The next morning General Hutchison, commanding the Tacloban field, told Dick to scout around over the area around Talcoban and see if he could find any sites that looked suitable for airdromes. Talcoban's capacity was definitely limited and the reconstruction of the old Jap field ten miles to the south at Dulag did not look too promising. Dick had hardly gotten off the ground before the radar station warned him of the presence of two Jap fighter planes in the vicinity and gave him their location and course. Bong intercepted, fired a couple of bursts, and chalked up two more victories. The whole combat was seen from Talcoban airdrome so there was no question about their being officially credited to him. I wired General Arnold:

> In accordance with my instructions, Major Richard Bong is trying to be careful, but the Nips won't do their part. On the twenty-seventh, five hours after arriving at Talcoban, Bong was again forced to defend himself and number thirty-one resulted. On the twenty-eighth, while looking for suitable localities for airdromes in the vicinity of Talcoban, he was assaulted by two more Nips who became numbers thirty-two and thirty-three. Unless he was bothered again today, this is his latest score.
>
> —KENNEY

Arnold answered a day or two later:

> Major Bong's excuses in matter of shooting down three more Nips noted with happy skepticism by this headquarters. In Judge Advocate's opinion, he is liable under Articles of War 122 (willful or negligent damage to enemy equipment or personnel).
>
> —ARNOLD

I posted copies of both messages on the Forty-ninth Group headquarters bulletin board.

On October 30, we had enlarged the Tacloban field enough to handle some more airplanes. I sent word to have another twenty P-38s flown up. They came up around midafternoon. About twenty miles from the field, they were warned of the approach of ten Japanese planes. The P-38s arrived just in time, shooting down six Nips and chasing the rest away.

Slim little Tommy McGuire, who first shot down a Jap plane on August 18, the year before, got one of the victims, his twenty-third. He landed, casually told his adoring crew chief to paint another Jap flag on the side of his plane, and remarked, "This is the kind of place I like, where you have to shoot 'em down so you can land on your own airdrome. Say, how many has Bong got now?" McGuire hadn't heard about the last pair that Dick had added to his score. Much to his annoyance, he found that his regular "eight behind" had suddenly become ten behind. Tommy rectified the situation early the next morning. Nine P-38s on a patrol spotted six Jap planes about fifteen minutes after take off. Four of the Nips didn't get away. Two of these were credited to Major Thomas McGuire of the 475th Fighter Group. His score was now twenty-five. "Well, at least I'm holding my own," said Tommy.

The race was resumed on November 10. While with the P-38s escorting our bombing attack on a Jap shipping convoy bringing troops into Ormoc Bay on the west coast of Leyte, Bong got number thirty-four, "defending himself" against a Jap fighter. Tommy McGuire, who remarked as he took off that morning that he was only going along to protect his interests, also shot down a Nip, his twenty-sixth—still eight behind.

That evening we got word of another Jap convoy out of Manila on the way to Leyte. The next morning the whole area was fogbound, but around noon we managed to get off an attack. Bong and McGuire resumed the race, Dick getting two more Jap fighters, making his score thirty-six. Tommy McGuire also got a pair, to hold his place at twenty-eight.

December 7 was a big day. Our troops made a landing at Ormoc, and the Jap aviators spent most of the day trying to interfere with the expedition. The landing was made in spite of incessant and determined enemy air attacks. Kamikaze attacks sank two of the destroyers convoying the troop movement. Three of our aircraft were shot down, but we rescued all three pilots. The Japs lost fifty-six aircraft, fighters, and bombers. One of the Jap bombers and one fighter fell before Dick Bong's guns. Score thirty-eight. Tommy McGuire got a couple of Nip fighters, holding his second-place position with thirty. The next two in runner-up positions were Jerry Johnson with twenty-three and Lieutenant Colonel Charles MacDonald, McGuire's commanding officer, with twenty.

CHAPTER 10

Medal of Honor

SHORTLY AFTER BONG WAS CREDITED with his thirty-sixth officially confirmed destruction of a Japanese airplane in combat, I decided it was time to see General MacArthur about a Medal of Honor. Dick already had every other American decoration for valor, and I had given him nothing since he had returned to the theater in September. I had been saving those victories for this very purpose. Now I figured that eight Jap aircraft destroyed in little more than a month, especially when Bong was supposed to shoot only in "self-defense," warranted some real recognition.

"General," I said as soon as I entered his office, "I want a Medal of Honor for Dick Bong."

MacArthur smiled as I handed him the citation I had prepared. He barely glanced at it, looked up, and said, "I've been wondering when you were going to bring this matter up. It's long overdue. I'll approve this citation and forward it to Washington right away.

It read:

> For conspicuous gallantry and intrepidity in action
> above and beyond the call of duty in the Southwest

Pacific Area from October 10 to November 15, 1944. Though assigned to duty as gunnery instructor and neither required not expected to perform combat duty, Major Bong voluntarily and at his own urgent request engaged in repeated combat missions, including unusually hazardous sorties over Balikpapan, Borneo, and in the Leyte area of the Philippines. His aggressiveness and daring resulted in his shooting down eight enemy airplanes during this period.

If I had waited until December 7 before writing up the citation, the number would have been ten instead of eight.

A couple of days later, General MacArthur told me he had just gotten word from Washington that the award had been made. I asked him to give it to Bong in a public ceremony on the Tacloban Airdrome. The general refused at first, saying that he was not running for any office and was not looking for publicity. He didn't want to break the precedent he had already established. He wanted to pin on the decoration in his office, as he had all the others he had personally handed out. I protested that the Forty-ninth Fighter Group was one of his favorite outfits. They all knew him, and he had met and personally congratulated all the top aces of the group. Also, Bong was their favorite, and I believe that they would be disappointed if they didn't see a show. Furthermore, I reminded him that a few months before he had publicly decorated me in Australia with the Distinguished Service Medal. He scowled at me, but his eyes were twinkling.

"Yes, and I've been wondering ever since why I did it," he said. "All right, George, I'll do it for you. When do you want the ceremony to take place?"

"Tomorrow noon on the strip at Tacloban," I replied. "I'll call for you and drive you out there myself." He nodded.

We lined up eight P-38s in a half circle, with the crews standing in front of them. Out in front of his guard of honor, consisting of twelve fighter pilots, all of whom had a dozen or more victories to their credit, stood Bong, speechless with stage fright and shaking like a leaf. In a sky full of Jap airplanes, all shooting in his direction, Dick would be as cool as a cucumber, but there in front of everybody, with the great MacArthur ready to decorate him with the highest award his country could give him, Bong was terrified.

The two advanced toward each other and Dick got his next shock when he saw the general beat him to the salute. I had forgotten to tell him that it was MacArthur's custom to salute the man he was decorating. Bong hurriedly recovered and returned the greeting.

Either MacArthur himself, or his public relations department, had prepared a nice little speech for him to go with the award. It had been given to the press several hours before and by this time had already been wired back to the

Major Richard I. Bong receives the Congressional Medal of Honor on the beach at Tacloban, Leyte Island, December 12, 1944.
PHOTO, JAMES E. LYNCH, JR.

MacArthur to Bong: "I now induct you into the society of the bravest of the brave . . . " PHOTO, U.S. AIR FORCE

United States. It read:

> Of all military attributes, the one that arouses the greatest admiration is courage. The Congress of the United States has reserved to itself the honor of decorating those among all who stand out as the bravest of the brave. It is this high and noble category, Major Bong, that you now enter as I pin upon your breast the Medal of Honor. Wear it as a symbol of the invincible courage you have displayed in mortal combat. My dear boy, may a merciful God continue to protect you—that is the prayer of your commander in chief.

It was a good speech, but MacArthur didn't use it. I don't know whether he even had a piece of paper in his pocket. I think that he looked at Bong, with his guard of honor, every one of whom he had met and had followed their careers, he realized that this was the cream of the crop of wonderful youngsters who had fought a good fight for him regardless of the odds during those long, lean years since he first saw them in New Guinea back in the summer of 1942. I believe, too, that he looked upon Dick, the lad he was about to decorate, as the symbol of modern American youth which had taken to the air in this latest of developments of the weapons of warfare. Maybe it was the background of P-38s that he knew so well, but something certainly inspired him that day.

As Bong finished returning his salute, the general stepped forward, put his two hands on Dick's shoulders, and gave what I still think is the greatest speech I have ever heard. It was only one sentence long, but it packed a world of meaning. Here it is:

> Major Richard Ira Bong, who has ruled the air from New Guinea to the Philippines, I now induct you into the society of the bravest of the brave, the wearers of the Congressional Medal of Honor of the United States.

A vast sigh whispered around the airdrome. Two thousand spectators—GIs, airmen, war correspondents, Filipinos—had forgotten to breathe during that one-sentence tribute to America's ace of aces. How could you better describe the top ace of the Pacific than to sweep over two thousand miles of geography where he had "ruled the air," and how could you better refer to the Medal of Honor than by calling its wearers "the society of the bravest of the brave"?

MacArthur pinned the medal on Dick's chest, shook hands, the two exchanged salutes, and the ceremony was over. Vastly relieved, Bong ducked into the crowd and slipped over to the Forty-ninth Group officers' mess, to see what they had for lunch. He had been so worried that morning that he had missed breakfast.

General Hutchison, commanding the air units at

Tacloban and Dulag, Lieutenant Colonel Walker, the Forty-ninth Group commander, "Jerry" Johnson, Bob Morrisey, and several of the headquarters staff were there. They had finished lunch just before going to Bong's decoration ceremony and had just returned.

"Say, when do we eat?" said Dick as he entered the hut. He had taken off his medal and put it in his shirt pocket for safekeeping. It wouldn't do to try to strut his decoration in front of all these friends of his. They had already seen him get it, so why try to impress them? "I'm hungry. I had to hurry from Dulag this morning and didn't get any breakfast except a cup of coffee and a little cheese sandwich."

"Why, we had lunch before we went out to the field," said Walker. "How about some bread and a can of tuna fish? I'm afraid that's about all we've got left. It's over there on the table. Help yourself."

Dick opened the can and spread the tuna fish about an inch thick between two huge slices of bread. He munched happily for a minute or two and then remarked, "Boy, this tastes good, but you ought to see how my mom fixes tuna fish." Jerry Johnson interrupted, "Dick, I've got an idea. After the war, I think my wife and I will take a trip to Wisconsin and look you up and stay with you for a week or so and see about that cooking you're always talking about. Now for breakfast I'd like to have a big batch of fried chicken or maybe . . ."

Richard Ira Bong wearing the Medal of Honor. PHOTO, U.S. AIR FORCE

107

"Chicken?" said Bong. "Mom can really fix a chicken, and she makes gravy for it that . . ."

"Don't forget, I want it fried," said Johnson.

"Aw, now, wait a minute," said Dick. "Let me tell you how she fixes it. First she cuts it up, then she rubs some butter over it and sprinkles some flour over the pieces. Then she gets a cup of cream and puts the whole works in a frying pan, and . . ."

"I told you I wanted it fried. That's okay Dick, go ahead and tell me the rest." He settled back in his chair as Bong finished the detailed description of how his "mom fixed a chicken."

No one thought to mention the relatively unimportant episode that had just taken place out on the Tacloban airstrip that day.

CHAPTER 11

Bong and McGuire

ON DECEMBER 15, I DROVE TO DULAG to see how the airdrome construction was coming along. We'd had a lot of trouble with it from the start as the ground was soft originally and hadn't been hardened up any since the rainy season began around the first of November. We had barely enough parking space off the single runway for MacDonald's 475th Fighter Group of P-38s. I had told the engineers to truck in some gravel or cracked stone to fill in and enlarge the field so we could have some room to disperse our planes, which were lined up, wing tip to wing tip, on each side of the one-hundred-foot-wide runway.

I stopped to chat with some of the 475th pilots who were looking over their airplanes preparatory to going out on patrol. One of them told me that Bong and McGuire had gone out on a Nip-hunting expedition together that morning and had shot down a Jap plane. He said that they had been back about half an hour and were now over at McGuire's quarters. I had told Dick he could be a free lance and go with any outfit that would have him, but he had generally strung with his old Ninth Squadron of the Forty-ninth Fighter

109

Group, then operating out of the field at Tacloban, twenty miles north of Dulag. I wondered what he was doing flying with the 475th.

I got in my jeep and drove over to the hut where McGuire was living with two or three other members of his squadron. I opened the door without knocking and walked in. Bong and McGuire, naked as the day they were born, were standing in a pair of tin washtubs, scrubbing each other's backs. They turned around, grinned rather sheepishly, and reached for towels. I sat down, and as they dressed, asked them what they had been doing that morning. I wanted to know if that rumor I had heard about the Japs losing a couple more airplanes was true and also, how come Bong and McGuire were now flying together? McGuire took on the task of spokesman while Bong sat there grinning and nodding confirmation as the story unfolded.

"You see, General," said Tommy, "that Forty-ninth gang up at Tacloban didn't want Dick going along with them any more, as he was stealing too many Nips from them, so he came down here to see if we would let him fly with the 475th. We figured we were good enough so we could take care of our own interests along the line, so we said it would be okay. This morning he saw me getting ready to take off for a look at the Jap fields over on Mindanao and suggested that he go along. I had a hunch I shouldn't have let him come with me, but I had to be polite, so I gave in. We picked up a wingman apiece and took off.

Major Dick Bong and Major Tommy McGuire, the two leading American aces, November, 1944. PHOTO, U.S. AIR FORCE

"We cruised all over the island looking for something to shoot at, but the bombers and strafers have about cleaned the place out. We had just decided to call it off and go home when we spotted a couple of Oscars just ahead of us, near Pamubulon Island, flying low just over the treetops. They were on my side and I figured maybe Dick hadn't seen them so I barely whispered over the radio to my wingman to follow me and dive to take one of the Nips. One nice burst, and down he goes. I turn to knock off the other Oscar, but this eavesdropping Bong had heard me talking to my wingman and had located the Nip. Before I could get in position, I saw him blow up, and Bong pulls up alongside of me waggling his wings and grinning at me, like the highway robber he is. That makes him thirty-nine and me thirty-one. I'm still eight behind. I'll bet when this war is over, they'll call me Eight Behind McGuire."

Colonel MacDonald, the 475th Group commander, whose score was now up to twenty-three, and a couple of other pilots had come in while McGuire was talking. We all laughed at Tommy and his pretense of being sore at Bong. No one could help liking Bong, even his closest rival for the position of top ace, Tommy McGuire, and no one could help liking McGuire, least of all Dick Bong.

Tommy said they had a cold turkey that was only half gone and if I'd stay for lunch, he'd see that I'd get my share of it if he had to tie both of Dick's hands. "Bing Bong," as the kids had started to nickname him, had acquired quite a reputation as a trencherman.

I accepted the invitation and stayed for lunch. How they happened to have a turkey was really none of my business. I knew they hadn't gotten any Army issue of rations that even resembled a turkey, or I would have seen one at my own mess, but I resolved to make judicious inquiries and in

Dick with his 39th flag, December, 1944.

case some neighboring Filipino complained about one of his turkeys being liberated, to pay him for it and then forget the whole thing. As long as I was eating some plunder, I really was an accessory and should accept some responsibility in the matter.

I stayed around after lunch for the next couple of hours talking airplanes, combat tactics, and how the war looked to be going, with my two top scorers and most of the rest of McGuire's squadron, who kept dropping in, and finally told them that I had work to do and couldn't hang around wasting my time gossiping with them any longer. I thanked Tommy for the lunch and said to let me know the next time they had a meal like this one so I could get in on it while it was hot. I had enjoyed myself thoroughly but had made up my mind that Bong was going home as soon as he made it an even forty.

That same day our troops landed at San Jose on the island of Mindoro and the engineers started at once to build an airdrome just outside the town. The Japs didn't like the idea at all, as it would put us too close to their big airdrome complexes around Manila and at Clark Field, about fifty miles to the northwest. Day and night our troops were subjected to air raids, and we took to maintaining fighter patrols over the San Jose area, while our bombers and strafers plastered the Jap fields on Luzon.

On the seventeenth, McGuire allowed Bong to join his

squadron on patrol over San Jose. It looked like an uneventful mission until, just as McGuire was about to signal the squadron to go home before they got too low on fuel, a couple of Jap fighters were seen coming in from the north below them. Neither of the two Nips got away. Dick took one and McGuire downed the other. Bong had his fortieth and Tommy his thirty-second. I sent word to Bong to fly his airplane to Tacloban and leave it there. Also that he was not to fly in combat before seeing me, in a couple of days, when I was due back from a trip to Hollandia.

When I landed at Tacloban a day or two later, they told me a story that confirmed my decision to send Bong home. That morning one of the Forty-ninth Group pilots had taken Bong's plane up for a test flight, as one of the engines had been worked on following Dick's report that it had been running a bit rough when he brought it up from Dulag. The pilot had just about cleared the airdome and had climbed to a little more than a thousand feet when one of the engines burst into flames. The pilot immediately took to his parachute, landing in Leyte Gulf about a hundred feet offshore, where he was picked up by one of our rescue boats, none the worse for the wear. The P-38, with thirty-six little Jap flags on the side of the fuselage, plunged into the bay and sank.

Every officer and enlisted man on the field who saw the take-off and the crash recognized the airplane and thought that Bong was flying it. They all held their breaths when they saw the pilot bail out, and there was a headlong rush of at least a hundred worried men to the beach, ready to swim out after him. The relief expressed by everyone that crowded around me to tell me the story and the questions about how long Bong was going to continue in the theater told me the answer plainer than ever. I told them to quit worrying, as forty victories were enough, and I was going to order Dick home, to be acclaimed as the American ace of aces.

CHAPTER 12

I Take Bong Out of Combat

I SENT FOR DICK to tell him he was definitely and finally out of the combat and going home. His official score was now forty enemy aircraft destroyed in the air. Everyone knew that he had knocked down at least that many more that he had reported destroyed but for which there were no witnesses. They had nearly all been shot down over the ocean, so we could not even find the wreckage to serve as evidence. If Bong said he had shot down a Jap, we believed him, but the rules called for a confirming witness or definite evidence before official credit for the victory could be given. He was eight ahead of Major Tommy McGuire, my number-two ace, who was tied with the top score of the leading American fighter pilot in the European theater. It was improbable that anyone would equal Bong's score before the war ended in Europe or in the Pacific. Forty was a score that would be tops for any American aviator for all time. It was doubtful whether any future war would last long enough for anyone to get as many as forty official victories again.

Since arriving in the Southwest Pacific Theater, Dick had flown 146 combat missions and had nearly four hundred hours of combat time. In some theaters, pilots were allowed to go home for keeps after twenty-five combat missions.

Dick wanted to make it an even fifty, and I sympathized with him. I didn't think there was a Jap in the whole empire who could get Bong's airplane in his gun sights, but ever since Neel Kearby and Tommy Lynch had been lost, General Arnold kept sending me radio messages and letters asking me to take Dick out of combat before it was too late. General MacArthur had mentioned several times that he would hate to see Major Bong listed among those shot down. He knew Bong, had followed his string of victories, and liked the kid. The whole Forty-ninth Fighter Group and, in fact, the whole Fifth Air Force wanted me to send him home. I, too, was beginning to worry about sending that pitcher to the well too often. After all, he had repaid Uncle Sam many times for what it had cost to make a fighter pilot out of him. Why not send him home and let him marry the girl and be a live hero? There was no use letting him plead with me about staying in combat. It was too easy for me to give in, so as soon as he showed up, I put the cards on the table.

He was going home. There would be no more combat and that was that, so I didn't want any more arguments. Forty was a nice even number, and he was to quit talking about fifty or any other number. I wanted him to go home while he was still in one piece, marry Marjorie, and start thinking about raising a lot of towheaded Swedes like himself.

Dick listened without saying a word until I had finished. You could see that a lot of things were going on in that head of his. A country boy who liked his family. Of course, he wanted some more of Mom's cooking; he wanted to hunt and fish with his dad; he liked to chat with his friends in Poplar. He was crazy about a girl named Marjorie and wanted to marry her as soon as the war was over. At the same time he hated to quit chasing Jap airplanes as long as the war was on, but if I wanted him to go home it was all right. He knew that I liked him and was trying to take care of him. He would do what I asked.

"O.K., General, I'll quit arguing and go home whenever you say," he said. "But I'd like to make one more trip to Mindoro and check over a couple of guys in the Seventh Squadron of that Forty-ninth Group who need a little more gunnery instructions."

I knew that what he really wanted to go over there for was to say good-bye to the old gang. That was natural. Of course he should.

"As a matter of fact, I think it is a good idea," I replied. "I am going over there on an inspection trip myself tomorrow, and I'll need some fighter escort on the way, as we will pass over a couple of hundred miles of Jap-held territory. I'd rather have you than a squadron of any other fighter pilots, so borrow a P-38 from someplace and come along. I'll let you know when I'm ready. In the meantime, better get your stuff together and packed for that trip home."

With Bong out of combat, McGuire expected that his opportunity had come, but there just weren't any more Nips to be found south of Luzon. The incessant airdrome attacks had just about depopulated every Jap field south of Manila. With our new airdrome under construction in Mindoro, however, the gang was looking forward to hitting Nips around Manila and Clark Field.

On the afternoon of December 22, we opened that campaign with more than two hundred bombers, strafers, and fighters destroying nearly 125 Jap planes on the ground and shooting down eight out of the nine airborne fighters that tried to interfere. We had no losses. Our attacks the next day cost the enemy another thirty-three in combat and fifty-eight more on the ground. We lost a P-38.

On Christmas Day, our attack was intercepted by seventy Nip fighters. It cost them thirty-nine. We lost five P-38s but recovered three of the pilots. Tommy McGuire, leading his squadron which had just moved to Mindoro, shot down three of them to bring his score to thirty-five. For the first time the "eight behind" jinx was out of the way.

The next day we raided Clark Field again. Only twenty Jap fighters contested this time. Our escorting fighters shot down thirteen of them. Three of the victims fell to Tommy

McGuire, back in there still leading his squadron. That ran his total up to thirty-eight, now only two behind Bong's record of forty.

The next morning I sent for McGuire. I told him I was taking him off flying, as he looked tired to me. Tommy protested, "General, I never felt better in my life. I've gained five pounds in the last month. Besides, I'm only two behind, and . . ."

"That's just it," I said. "You are tired, and you won't be rested enough to fly again until I hear that Bong has arrived back in the United States and has been greeted as the top-scoring ace of the war. As soon as I get that news, you can go back to work. If I let you go out today, you are liable to knock off another three Nips and spoil Dick's whole party. What do you want him to do, land at San Francisco and have everyone say, 'Hello, Number Two, how's the war going?'"

Tommy laughed, but he didn't want to spoil anything for Dick, so it was O.K. He'd relax, take it easy, get a lot of sleep for a few days, and then—he hoped the Japs wouldn't run out on us for a while yet. By the way, when was Bong going home?

"I'm taking him over to Mindoro on an inspection trip tomorrow or the next day," I replied, "and I'll see that he is loaded on an airplane bound for the United States as soon as we get back. I'm going to make a courier out of him, with top priority, so my estimate is that you should be sufficiently recovered in about a week to go back into combat.

Now that that is settled, how about having lunch with me?"

Since I had acquired the former chef of the St. Francis Hotel in San Francisco as my cook, everyone liked to be invited to my mess. Tommy said he sure hoped my estimate as to the duration of his "illness" was correct, and he couldn't think of anything he'd rather do in the meantime than eat a meal with me.

A couple of days later, shortly after daybreak, with Bong in a borrowed P-38 acting as my escort, I took off to inspect the new airdromes around San Jose, Mindoro.

All the way from Tacloban airfield in Leyte to Mindoro, Dick's P-38 crisscrossed back and forth above my B-17. Those keen blue eyes of his would have spotted any enemy airplanes miles away and my own machine gunners would have been merely spectators at the combat. However, the trip was without incident, as I had expected, or I wouldn't have taken the chance on his getting into another fight. We landed at the San Jose field shortly after noon and taxied into the parking area.

As I shut off the engines, the siren sounded, and over the radio I heard the warning "Red alert." We hadn't had time to get our radar warning net in place, so this meant that in ten minutes at the most Jap airplanes would be over the area.

Colonel "Jerry" Johnson, in command of the Forty-ninth Fighter Group, led the alert squadron into the air to make the interception. It took place almost directly over the field at around fifteen thousand feet. Johnson, the crack shot, opened that attack. The leader of the Jap formation was set on fire by Johnson's first burst, and as he pulled over to take on another victim, the Jap leader pilot, unable to stand the flames, jumped overboard. The Nips didn't wear parachutes or at least never used them over our territory as it was against their code to be taken prisoner, so the plunge meant certain death.

The Jap pilot hit flat on the steel plank surface of the airdrome about a hundred feet from where Dick and I were standing. It was not a pretty sight. I watched for Bong's reaction. I had predicted a long while ago that if he ever found out that he was not shooting clay pigeons, I would have to take him out of combat. This was a nice kid. He was no killer, and his pet peeve against the newspapermen was that they kept referring to him as the "pilot with the most kills." As he watched Johnson's victim plunge to his death, I believe it was the first time he realized that he, Dick Bong, had been responsible for many similar occurrences. He walked over to some bushes at the edge of the field and for the next five minutes was violently ill.

There wasn't anything I could do, so I stood there waiting, more than ever convinced that tonight was the time for Dick to start home. He came over to me. The lad was quite evidently upset. He was no longer the happy-go-lucky, snub-nosed, towheaded country boy. He had definitely aged in the last few minutes. This was a rough, dirty game that he had been playing, and I instinctively sensed that he didn't want any more of it.

"General," he asked, " when are you going back to Tacloban?"

"About seven o'clock tonight," I replied. "We will land about nine thirty."

"Well, sir," he went on, "the group here could probably use my P-38, and as you are making a night flight back, you won't need any fighter escort, so if you don't mind I'll go back with you."

"Certainly, Dick," I said. "Be here at seven thirty, and in the meantime, I'll radio back that you have a seat on that transport plane leaving for the United States at midnight. Also, I'll have a letter to General Arnold ready for you to deliver to him in Washington. That will make you a courier and give you top priority all the way back. In the letter I am going to ask him to let you go home to get married and have a honeymoon. After that I'm asking him to send you to the Matériel Division in Dayton, Ohio, to learn something about jet engines and jet airplanes and then transfer you to the Lockheed plant in Burbank, California, where they are producing the new P-80 jet fighter. You were talking the other day how you would like to play with a jet, so this will give you a chance to do it. How about it? Does this sound all right or is there something else you would rather do?"

A couple of big tears welled out in spite of his trying to

hold them back. He brushed them off hastily and rubbed his eyes as though some dust had gotten into them.

"Oh, General, that's fine. I want to keep on flying. I just don't . . . Sure I'd like to try flying a jet. I'll bet they are pretty hot. I . . ."

I put my arm over his shoulder and said, "Aw, shut up. I'll see you at seven thirty, and don't be late."

He left for the Forty-ninth Fighter Group Headquarters while I got a letter ready for him to take to Washington. It read:

> I am sending this letter to you by Major Richard Bong, your top-ranking fighter ace, whose score I have stopped at forty. Bong is still capable of shooting down Nips and is not war weary by any stretch of the imagination, but I believe that forty is a good number for him to stop on.
>
> At the time you suggested that he be withdrawn from active combat I not only agreed but sent him home to learn the job of gunnery instructor in order to give my fighter youngsters the benefit of the latest developments in the United States along that line. Working at my combat replacement and training center at Nadzab, he has done a superb job, and the combat results achieved by our fighter pilots during the past couple of months are a real tribute to the value of his instruction.
>
> Along about the first of October, Bong informed me that all fighter replacements now coming in had taken

the same course that he had attended and that there was nothing that he could teach them. He then asked to be attached to the various units at the front to bring such of those pilots who had not taken the course up to date. As you know, from some of the more or less facetious radiograms that we have exchanged on the subject, this resulted in Bong's score being pushed from twenty-eight to forty. In spite of a suggestion made recently in *Time* magazine, none of the official Nips to Bong's credit were setups. He has invariably selected the leader of the enemy formation in order to break up the show and make it easier for his wingmen to add to their scores. He has more than deserved every one of the decorations he wears.

The reason that I am sending him home is that he is so popular with the personnel of the Fifth Air Force and so many of them have begun to worry about the possibility of his being shot down that I can no longer take the chance of the loss of morale that would result in case he become a casualty.

Bong is particularly anxious to get in on the development of the jet-propelled fighter, and I believe that, if possible, he should be given that opportunity. With his wide combat experience against every type of aircraft the Japanese possess, he should be invaluable for the development of any special changes in tactics that would result in shifting over to a radically different type of fighter. Bong is a cool, level-headed thinker. From talking to him, you get the idea that his thinking apparatus works a little slowly, but it has the tremendous virtue of being right most of the time. I would like to see him sent to the Matériel Division and given every opportunity to learn something about the jet engine and the airplane. While he is not now capable of being a project officer for this airplane, he should be of real value in test work and development tactics.

I imagine that he will be of considerable value to you for the Air Force publicity purposes before he goes to the Matériel Division, and another matter that will delay his assignment there is the fact that the girl he is engaged to gets out of school in the middle of January. Bong blushingly admits that he would like to get married about that time, so please don't let any of his public appearances interfere with his appearance at the church in Superior, Wisconsin.

I am sending Bong home as a courier in order to ensure that he arrives in the United States as your top-ranking ace. I have taken out additional insurance on this matter by putting Major Tommy McGuire on the ground for a week to give him a rest, which he really doesn't need. and also to keep him from passing Bong's score too soon. In the past two days Tommy has shot down seven Nips, bringing his score to thirty-eight. The way this lad takes out enemy aircraft in batches of three and four makes it almost certain that in the next fight he will either tie or pass Bong.

Sincerely

George C. Kenney
Lieutenant General U.S.A.
Commanding

After finishing my inspection and conferring with General Whitehead in regard to the part the Fifth Air Force was to play in the coming operations in Luzon, I went down to the strip to take off. Bong was waiting there for me. The trip back was uneventful. Dick didn't act as though he wanted to talk, so after a few remarks to try to make him feel at ease, I said I guessed I'd take a nap and promptly dozed off until we landed on the strip at Tacloban.

Just before midnight that night, December 29, 1944, armed with my letter to General Hap Arnold and six bottles of Coca-Cola that I managed to scare up at the last minute, Major Richard Ira Bong boarded the Air Transport Command flight back home. I said, "So long, Dick, I hope to see you again before too long. Say hello to your mom and dad for me."

I never saw him again.

CHAPTER 13

The Race Ends

ON THE AFTERNOON OF JANUARY 6, 1945, the word came in that Major Bong had arrived in the United States and had been hailed as America's ace of aces. The farm boy from Poplar, Wisconsin, had become a national hero. His picture was in every newspaper and magazine in the country. Every youngster aspiring to fly knew the story of his exploits and could give a blow-by-blow description of how his score had mounted since that December day in 1942, when he had scored his first victory. There was a human-interest story, too. Everyone seemed to know that there was a girl named Margie in the picture, and there was a story about a wedding to be covered as soon as they could find out from the couple when and where it was to take place.

I sent for Tommy McGuire to have dinner with me that evening. After the meal I told him that I believed he was now sufficiently rested and could go back to work shooting down Nips. I begged him, however, to take it easy and not try to get all the Jap airplanes left in his first combat. If he would just play a hit-and run game and get them one at a time, he would live through the war, but if he started pressing or got careless, his luck might run out. I didn't want to have to write a letter back to his parents.

Tommy assured me that he would be careful. He said that the next morning he and Major Rittmayer, a visiting P-38 pilot from the Thirteenth Air Force, who had four to his credit, were planning to take along a couple of youngsters who had just arrived in the squadron for a sweep over the Jap airdromes on the islands of Cebu and Negros to see if they could stir up something. We said goodnight.

On the morning of the seventh, McGuire and Rittmayer and the two new lads took off on the mission as scheduled. Cruising at 2,000 feet to make sure that nothing escaped them, they combed the islands, scanning every runway and dispersal area. Over Negros Island, they finally sighted a lone Jap fighter that had just lifted off the runway and was flying at about two hundred feet. McGuire led his flight to the attack. The Nip turned sharply to the left and quickly maneuvered into position on Rittmayer's tail. Rittmayer called to Tommy to "get that Jap off my tail" just as the Nip poured a burst of machine-gun fire into him.

McGuire frantically whipped his plane around in a vertical bank to try to get his guns on the Nip and save his friend Rittmayer. He didn't have the time to jettison the big 160-gallon auxiliary gasoline tanks suspended from his wings. Tommy had constantly preached to everyone in his squadron never to try a fast turn at a low altitude without first getting rid of the auxiliary tanks, but now in his anxiety to help his friend, he violated his own instructions. At that low altitude and with the heavy load he was carrying, it was a thousand to one that he couldn't make it, but Tommy took that chance. The P-38 shuddered in the vertical position, hesitated momentarily, and spun into the ground. An explosion, a blaze of flame and smoke, and Major Thomas McGuire, number-two ranking ace of the war, had changed his role from that of contestant for the position of top ace to a more glorious one, a member of those whom St. John said, "Greater love hath no man than this, that a man lay down his life for his friends."

As McGuire's plane crashed, the Jap pilot fired another burst into Rittmayer's already crippled P-38 and Rittmayer went down in flames. The Nip ducked behind a hill and got away. He probably never realized how much damage he had done. The two green youngsters, who had gone on the flight to get experience, in trying to stay with their two leaders, had gotten out of position and couldn't catch the Jap before he had disappeared from sight.

An accident had deprived us of a great aviator and leader. Tommy hadn't had a bullet hole in his airplane for more than a year. No Jap shot him down. I don't believe there was a Jap in the world could have shot Tommy down, but his loss was one of the worst blows I took in the whole war. I wrote to his father that night. It was not an easy letter to write.

We named a field in Mindoro after Tommy. Later he was to get a posthumous Congressional Medal of Honor and have an air force base in his home state of New Jersey name after him, but the race of the aces was now over.

CHAPTER 14

Last Flight

ON THE SAME DAY that I received the news of the loss of Tommy McGuire, a courier delivered to me a letter from General Arnold. It told of getting the letter I had given Bong when he left home and Hap's plans for Dick. Hap's letter read:

Dear George:

I received your letter relative to Bong and have had a long talk with him, and I think you are right in sending Bong home. He can be of great value to us here.

Present plan for Bong's employment is that he will be on detached service at Superior, Wisconsin, until about the first week in February, after which he will go on twenty-one days' leave, and on termination of this leave will report to Dayton for duty in connection with jet-propelled airplanes. He has done a magnificent job and we should capitalize on his experience.

Yours sincerely

H. H. ARNOLD
COMMANDING GENERAL
ARMY AIR FORCES

Hap did even better than his letter indicated. The detached service at Superior was to all intents and purposes a vacation. Dick's duties were to check in once in a while to see if there were any messages or instructions for him. This lasted until February 10, 1945, when he and Marjorie were married in the Concordia Lutheran Church in Superior. The Reverend Paul Boe, a friend of both bride and groom, officiated. The church was crowded to capacity, with many others waiting outside to see and greet the pair when they came out after the ceremony. Besides the two families, all of Dick's old friends from Poplar were on hand along with classmates of both Dick and Marjorie from Superior State Teacher's College to wish them well and help with the rice and old shoes.

That afternoon they drove to Minneapolis, where they spent the night, and the next day flew to Los Angeles, where they spent most of their honeymoon. Dick had told General Arnold that he wanted to go to California on his honeymoon and while there visit the Lockheed Aircraft plant in Burbank, where the new jet fighter, the P-80, was being built, so Arnold had told him to report in to the Santa Monica Redistribution Center to pick up his orders for Wright Field, Ohio, in time to get there on April 6.

The honeymoon trip ended on April 6, when Major and Mrs. Bong arrived in Dayton, Ohio. Dick reported for duty at Wright Field, and then he and Marge went house hunting. They found a little house in the neighboring town of Osborn.

For the next two months, Bong absorbed all he could learn about jet engines and jet airplanes at the Flight Test Section of the Matériel Command at Wright Field. There was a lot to learn, as it was entirely different from the reciprocating engined, propeller-driven aircraft that he had been familiar with, but Dick was so interested that it was not long before he could give lectures on the subject. Marge, who was learning the job of housewife, was his most frequent audience.

By the first week in June, it was decided that Bong was sufficiently proficient to be transferred to the Lockheed plant, where he would test-flight the P-80 jet fighters that were just beginning to come off the production line. Dick had bought a car while on duty in Dayton, so he and Marjorie packed up and headed back to California, detouring first by way of Poplar and Superior, Wisconsin, for a couple of days of visiting with the Bongs and the Vattendahls.

It was August 7, 1945. I was on my way to the Kadena airstrip in Okinawa, to take off for Manila, when a radiogram, which had been relayed from there, was handed to me by my signal officer. I stopped thinking about the atomic bomb which the previous morning had wiped out Hiroshima, stopped speculating about the effect of the coming entry of Russia into the Pacific war, even stopped thinking of the capitulation of Japan which we all knew was due to take place in a few days. Wherever I landed, I found that the whole Fifth Air Force felt the same way. We had lost someone we were all fond of, someone that we had been glad to see out of combat and on his way home eight months before.

Major Richard Ira Bong of Poplar, Wisconsin, was dead. That was the message that had taken our minds off the war, the Japs, the A-bomb. He had met the best the Japanese Air Force could send against him for over two years and won, but now he had joined the long list of gallant airmen whose brilliant careers had been terminated by accident. His jet engine had "flamed out" and quit right after the take-off. After trouble developed, he deliberately stayed with the crippled aircraft in a successful attempt to steer it away from civilian housing. That selfless act cost him his life. By the time he took to his parachute, there was not enough altitude for it to function.

The formal military funeral was held two days later at Superior, Wisconsin, the place of his birth. The burial service was in the Poplar Cemetery later on that afternoon.

The body of America's ace of aces was flown back to Wisconsin in an Army transport plane escorted by eighteen fighters. Marjorie, his widow, Colonel K.C. McGregor, commanding officer of the Long Beach Army Air Base, an air-flight surgeon, and a group of military pallbearers accompanied the dead hero. To take part in the services a one-hundred-man military police company and a military band of thirty men were flown in from Chicago. From Washington, representing General Arnold, were Major General Fred L. Anderson, Brigadier General Gordon P. Saville, and Brigadier General Charles H. Caldwell.

Village President Lapole of Poplar ordered all flags in the town to be flown at half mast the day of the funeral.

Dick had made his last flight.

Epilogue

It was in May 1946, while I was on duty in New York as senior American representative on the Military Staff Committee of the United Nations, that I was requested to give the Memorial Day address and unveil a bust of Dick Bong at the State Capitol in Madison, Wisconsin. The bust was to be a gift to the state by the Wisconsin State Historical Society. I accepted.

I arrived in Madison the afternoon before the ceremony. That evening I attended a private unveiling of the bust at the Historical Society headquarters. Governor and Mrs. Goodland were there, Mr. and Mrs. Carl Bong, the parents, Mrs. Marjorie Bong, Dick's widow, and perhaps twenty others. We lined up in a double row facing the bust and waited for the sculptor to unveil it. The sheet was removed and there was complete silence for almost a full minute. It was a superb job. It was Dick Bong suddenly frozen in bronze.

I was standing there in the front row with Mrs. Dora Bong on my left and Carl Bong on my right. They were both almost speechless at the likeness. So was I. Suddenly some woman in the back row broke the silence. "Oh, isn't that a shame."

"What's a shame?" It was the mother now, fiercely demanding to know what was wrong with the likeness of her son. To her it was perfect, and she resented any derogatory comment as though it were a criticism of her boy.

"Why, the left eye squints a little," came the reply from the woman who had made the comment, and who, without realizing it, had set the stage.

"Of course it squints," scornfully but proudly answered the mother. "We gave him his first rifle when he was twelve years old."

I put my arm around her and hugged her.

About the Artist

Herb Kawainui Kane (pronounced KAH-ney) is an art historian and author with special interest in Hawaii and the South Pacific. He resides in rural South Kona on the island of Hawaii.

Kane's career has included advertising art, publishing art, architectural design, painting, writing, and sculpture. Clients include many private collectors, the Hawaii State Foundation on Culture and the Arts, the National Park Service, *National Geographic*, and major publishers of books and periodicals. His art has appeared on seven postage stamps for the U.S. Postal Service and many stamps for several Pacific nations. His books now in print are *Pele, Goddess of Hawaii's Volcanoes* (1987, revised 1995) and *Voyagers* (Whalesong Publishing, 1991), which includes 140 of his works in color. His latest book, *Ancient Hawaii*, was published in 1998. In 1984 Herb Kane was elected a Living Treasure of Hawaii.

About the Art

Herb Kane graciously donated the rights to use his painting "Dick Bong's 22nd Victory" to the Richard I. Bong World War II Heritage Center. It appears on the cover of this book. About the painting, he says:

> I was raised in both Hawaii and Wisconsin. My mother was from Marshfield, and I was a teenager

there during the war, when my dad was in the navy. Dick Bong was my hero as he was to all Wisconsin boys, and I always wanted to do something to memorialize him. Eventually, this resulted, late in life, in my doing the painting of him making his 22nd kill over the New Guinea coast.

Richard Bong, a quiet-spoken Wisconsin farm boy, became a terror in a P-38 Lightning during WWII. The leading American ace, with forty confirmed victories, he earned the Congressional Medal of Honor.

The superiority of Japanese fighters during the early part of the war was not challenged until Navy Hellcats and Corsairs and Army Lightnings and Thunderbolts arrived in the Pacific. Although not as maneuverable as the Zero, the P-38 Lightning was faster, more heavily armed (a 20mm cannon and four 50 caliber machine guns), could take more punishment, and was capable of longer range.

In 1944, Dick was flying P-38J-15-LO, A.A.F. Serial Number 42-103993. This is the plane I chose to paint. The number on the nose was usually the last three digits of the serial number, but the photos show the "993" smudged with solvent and re-stenciled "597." Several weeks later, Dick had a color photo of his fiancee glued to the pilot's nacelle and her name, "Marge," lettered alongside. News photos of the plane became familiar to millions, but he made no further victories with it. While he was on leave, it was wrecked by another pilot. Bong used several other P-38s, flying a total of 146 missions.